I0518522

Hemlock Gems

Memories

of

Jack C. Evans:

His Boyhood Days

In Hemlock

Copyright © 2025 by
Little Finger Lakes Center Press
All rights reserved

Permission to reproduce in any form
must be secured from the publisher
Photographs courtesy of Little Finger Lakes Center Historical
Committee
And Richmond Town Historian

Published by Little Finger Lakes Center Press
Hemlock, N.Y. 14466

Contents

Introducing Jack and His Family

John Cushing Evans – "Jack" – was born in Buffalo, New York, on March 4, 1918. He was the only child of James and Grace (Covey) Evans. When he was a toddler, he and his mother moved to Hemlock to live with her parents; his dad at that time was away from home serving in the Army.

When James Evans returned to New York from his war-time service, he joined Grace and Jack in Hemlock, where they rented a house at the southern end of Main Street. Mr. Evans worked for the postal service, and was gone from home for long stretches of time, traveling by rail through the eastern U.S. His long absences encouraged the family to make changes in their living arrangements. Before Jack started school, the Evans family moved into the home of Grace's parents on Main Street. The Covey home was on the east side of Main Street, two houses north of Clay Street.

Jack lived in the village until his graduation from high school in 1935. He had lots of friends and many boyhood adventures, of which he wrote fondly. He acknowledged that growing up in Hemlock "was fortunate for me, because I realize I would have missed elsewhere many of the impressive and rich experiences [of] a rural community."

John Covey, Grace's father, born in the opening year of the Civil War, had grown up on a farm south of Buffalo. He was fascinated by the new-fangled railroad and determined to find his place in its organization. In his early twenties he was married to Emma VanSice, and in due time they became parents of three children: George, Ansel, and Grace.

John was yet a young man when he'd earned the job of railroad engineer. For more than forty years he was master of the great steam locomotive – first on the Buffalo/Sayre, Pennsylvania run on the Lehigh mainline, then from 1919 as engineer on the Rochester run out of Hemlock.

Grandpa Covey's railroad experience enriched Jack's boyhood. He grew up in his grandfather's shadow: riding in the cab of the steam engine as a regular pastime; meeting and befriending rail workers; observing the operation of a large business; and absorbing all sorts of life-lessons.

In his seventies Jack sat down to write his remembrances. He deeply appreciated the experience of growing up in a small town, where he knew most of his neighbors and had many friends among his schoolmates. Jack's voice comes through loud and clear in these collected sketches: the boy he was in the nineteen-twenties and thirties, the little village where he spent his childhood, the everyday workings of the railroad; all these episodes are vividly and touchingly portrayed.

June 1923: Grace Covey Evans (Jack's mother), Jack, Ansel Covey (Grace's bother), Ralph Briggs (on fence) and his girlfriend (unnamed)

Cast of Characters:
Neighbors and Friends

Jacob York Baker was known by his initials "J.Y." He was a railway worker in the early nineteen-thirties when he boarded with the Evans family during the week. On the weekends he went home to his family in Manchester, which included his wife Leila and four daughters.

Harlan Becker, a school friend, was born March 13, 1918; he was nine days younger than Jack. His family lived north of the Evans family on Main Street. Everyone in his family had a name that began with the letter "H" – father, Harrison; mother, Hattie; daughter, Hazel; and Harlan. Bruce Wemett, Jack, and Harlan, were fast friends all through school.

Harlan left school without graduating to take a job driving truck for the Hemlock Coal Supply Company. He married in his early twenties and within a few years was the father of three young children: Sally, Larry, and Jack. The youngest was a month old in November 1942, when Harlan was killed in a road accident. The company truck he was driving skidded on an icy road, hit a pole, and overturned.

Sam Boyd was an interesting village character, a well-known teller of tall tales. He was in his early fifties, married, and the father of a young daughter. Sam lived in Honeoye, but spent a great deal of time at the Hemlock rail depot. The rural mail carrier for Hemlock and Honeoye, Sam also provided a "taxi service" for passengers arriving by train in Hemlock who needed to continue on to Honeoye. He called his jitney conveyance "the stage."

George Briggs, a man in his late fifties, was a "shirt-tail relation" to Jack – his daughter Emma was married to Jack's uncle Ansel Covey. George, who did odd-jobs around town including work at the railyard, was a widower and boarded with a local family.

Anna Bush and her daughter Phebe Gibbs were teachers in the rural schoolhouses of Livonia and Richmond. They lived a couple houses to the north of the Evans family; both were widows. Anna was in her middle-sixties; Phebe in her forties.

Mrs. Bush was an active participant in the life of the village: hosting WCTU meetings in her home, teaching Sunday school at the Methodist Church, and heading committees for the Grange. The *Livonia Gazette* recorded on August 7, 1925 that "Mrs. Anna Bush has a new Ford sedan." Noteworthy, for few women owned, or even drove, a car at that time.

Mrs. Bush's last year of teaching was 1931, when she taught the Curtis District, the rural school on Route 20A between Honeoye and Hemlock. Mrs. Gibbs taught at Hemlock into the 1950s.

Phebe Gibbs

Larry Button, who shared the *Times-Union* paper route with Jack, was three years older than Jack. His father, Clair, was the Station Master at Hemlock Depot. Mr. Button's duties included supervision of the section hands and other railroad employees; he was in over-all charge of schedules, ensuring that the trains ran on time.

Ken Coykendall, the Station Master's Assistant at the Hemlock Depot, lived on Main Street, in a house just two doors north of the Adams Road intersection. Likely, he walked to work. He was in his early thirties, newly married, and would become the father of two boys between 1930 and 1940: Mel and Larry.

Hugh and Gertrude Drain were in their late twenties, with an elementary-aged son, Carl. They lived in the house next door to Jack's family, on the south – on the corner of Clay Street. Mr. Drain, who worked at the hardware store downtown, was Jack's Scout leader. Mrs. Drain was known and appreciated by the neighborhood children for her oatmeal cookies.

Bill Fogarty, in his mid-fifties, had been a Livingston County Deputy Sheriff for a decade and a half. He was a well-known presence in the village, called upon for every contingency including car accidents and suicides. (In 1949 he would play a prominent role in searching for the kidnapper of eleven-year-old Joanne Lynn.) Bill was married; he and Blanche lived on Main Street, south of downtown; they had no children.

Bill Mallaber and his wife Hattie lived on Clay Street, just around the corner from Jack's home. They were in their mid-sixties, the parents of three grown daughters. He worked for the railroad as a carpenter and section hand, commuting to work in Buffalo from his Hemlock home by train. In the evenings he came home from Rochester Junction via handcar.

One night in late September 1933 Bill was on his way home when he was struck by the hit-and-run driver of a truck at the Livonia Center rail crossing. He died the next day in Genesee Hospital.

Dr. Harold Trott and his wife Hazel lived in the house on Main Street directly north of Jack's family home. They were in their early thirties and childless. (Their only child, Edward, would not be born until 1937, a couple years after Jack had graduated high school.)

Dr. Harold Trott

One contemporary remembered the doctor as a "ruddy-faced [man], stoutish; he had a small mustache, blue eyes, and black hair." All who knew him agreed that he had "a flair for conversation." He wore leg braces and walked with a noticeable limp due to an illness he suffered in his late teens. Dr. Trott set up his medical practice in Hemlock in 1925, a year after graduating from McGill College in Canada.

His overriding interest, other than medicine, was for flying. He owned and flew a small plane, published a magazine reporting on helicopters. After he'd been in Hemlock a few years, he established an airport at the top of the hill north of the village, with a four-bay hangar. Dr. Trott participated in Flying Meets across the state. He was present at a meet in upstate New York in 1928 where Amelia Earhart was present, and made a home movie recording of the event, which has been preserved.

Charlie Wesley, born in the spring of 1919, was a year younger than Jack. The boys were both in the same Boy Scout troop. The troop leader, Hugh Drain, was Charlie's uncle; Hugh's sister Elizabeth was Charlie's mother. His dad was Murray Wesley. Charlie had a younger sister, Gladys. The Wesley family lived on Main Street, a few houses north of Jack.

When he grew up Charlie married Betty Belcher; they lived in a house on the west side of Main Street at the top of the hill north of Hemlock. Charlie and Betty had two sons: elder son Don, and younger son Richard, who became a New York State Supreme Court Judge.

Bruce Wemett, Jack's best friend, was a few months older than Jack, the son of Clarence and Ada (Jennings) Wemett. He lived a few houses south of the Evanses on the same side of Main Street. The boys were in the same class at Hemlock School. He had an older sister, Ruth, and an older brother, Norris. His younger siblings were twins, Mark and Mary.

Bruce's dad Clarence was the owner of the Hemlock Hardware, as well as the local distributor for the Shell Oil Company. In the winter of Bruce's senior year of high school his mother died of pneumonia.

Fellow Students: Jack's high school class included Ralph Barnard, Glenn Barnhardt, Elizabeth Caskey, Jack Connor, Robert Crane, Harold Edwards, John Jones, Ray Morrell, Anne and Carmello Muscato, Lucille Paul, Elizabeth Schoonover, and Bruce Wemett.

Hemlock High School: Jack graduated in 1935

A Boy's Kingdom

Flight
1928: Age ten

My earliest recollection of airplanes came about because our next-door neighbor, Dr. Trott, possessed a fervent interest in the introduction of the private airplane. A few models of private planes came onto the market following WWI. Dr. Trott probably purchased his first plane around 1925. He fashioned a small airfield north of the village on the high ground between the two valleys. It took a stretch of the imagination to have called this field an airport. It was definitely a field – a hay field with nothing obvious to mark a landing strip. In one corner of this forty-acre field, Dr. Trott erected a small wooden structure for a hangar, painted white. The building had three or four barn doors that could be rolled to one side to permit a small plane, and possibly a second and a third, to enter and exit. Atop the roof of the small hangar was a vertical staff supporting a yellow windsock.

The decade of the twenties saw the origin of "barnstorming" – where the pilot of a small plane would travel around the country appearing at fairs and carnivals and perform an exhibition of stunt flying and parachute jumping. I was ten years old when a barnstormer flew into town with his WWI surplus warplane, the venerable "Jenny." He must have landed about the time school was dismissed. Two or three of my classmates and I joined a number of curious grown-ups to hurry to the airport to see this

9

visitor and his plane. The Jenny was a two-seater, open cockpit, wood frame, fabric-covered biplane powered by an in-line, six-cylinder, water-cooled engine driving a single, two bladed wooden propeller. Quantities of these planes were manufactured in Hammondsport, New York, in the plant of Glenn Curtiss, who was one of the renowned pioneers of the airplane industry.

(My uncle George was employed at the Curtiss plant during WWI. As a souvenir of the war and of the planes manufactured at the Curtiss plant, George gave his father – my grandfather – a novel ashtray that was prominently displayed in our living room. It was made from a highly polished aluminum aircraft engine piston, four inches in diameter, cut in such a way that it provided a pair of supports for a cigar.)

So, back to the barnstorming pilot. The aviator flying the Jenny was an army veteran who had flown the same breed of fighter plane during the war. It was clear that he was very proud of his airplane and his ability to fly it. The fuselage had an American flag, also various symbols and decorations, emblazoned on it that were a mystery to me, a ten-year-old observer. The pilot wore a brown leather flight jacket and a matching leather helmet with goggles to pull down over his eyes if needed in flight.

As the little cluster of the hometown curious gathered around his plane, the barnstorming pilot beamed his approval and offered to demonstrate his wares in flight. He directed the sightseers to move back from his craft and ordered his assistant to prepare for starting the engine.

The assistant, wearing a pair of gloves, took his stance beneath the propeller. At a signal from the pilot in the cockpit, he reached upward grasping one end of the propeller, and throwing most of his weight on it, he pulled it down through one compression stroke of the engine. This maneuver was repeated several times in succession to fill the cylinder chambers with an air-fuel mixture before turning on the ignition.

The pilot then shouted a command, "Contact!" which signaled that the ignition switch was closed – in the next pull-down stroke of the prop the engine was going to fire. This downward stroke was the critical one, and a hazardous one for the assistant. He had to make certain that his arms and upper body would be clear of the whirling propeller when the engine fired, for serious injury could occur if he were struck. In this instance the assistant performed his task flawlessly and the engine burst into its resounding clatter.

The pilot waved to the spectators, advanced the throttle, taxied off to one end of the field. He turned the plane around, then roared down one side of the airfield, taking off into the wild blue yonder. But the blue yonder in this case was at a very low altitude, only about a hundred feet off the ground. He banked the plane in a tight half circle and proceeded to make repetitive figure eight patterns over the airfield.

I was amazed at how he could bank that plane at forty-five degrees around the arcs and flatten it out on the straight legs of the figure eights! The spectators, including me, stood entranced on the field with the Jenny roaring past in one direction and then curving back to roar past in the opposite direction. I was awestruck; I haven't witnessed anything quite like it since.

Upon landing the plane the pilot addressed his audience, "I bet you haven't seen anyone do a figure eight within the bounds of your airfield before."

Obviously, we hadn't!

In the nineteen-thirties, there were the Air Meets in which the aviators and their planes from far and near gathered at small airports to show off their planes, take up passengers, demonstrate parachute jumps, perform aerial aerobatics, drop small bags of flour at ground targets, and other stunts.

Dr. Trott's airfield was one of the meccas of these early airplane enthusiasts. The Air Meets were usually held on Sundays with the festivities going on from mid-morning until the early evening. The airplane was a new phenomenon; it invited curiosity and visions of the future – and so they came, the oldsters, the youngsters, and all ages in between. The whole show was free entertainment for the entire family.

On these Sundays the highway next to the airfield would be jammed with parked cars, necessitating a deputy sheriff or two to control the traffic. The crowd, attired in their Sunday best, gawked at the planes in the air and on the ground. A refreshment stand served the patrons hot dogs and soft drinks. Souvenirs addressing the Aviation Age were the rage of the day. To a youth like me it was all fun – exciting and unforgettable. As the Great Depression deepened and the novelty of the airplane diminished, the Air Meets faded into history.

The Handcar
1932: Fourteen

Bruce had brought a flashlight. As we stepped along the railroad ties beside the freight platform, he flashed the light on and off, directing the beam under the platform.

"There she is!" he exclaimed as if he had discovered a cache of gold.

My eyes beheld a bright yellow, three-wheeled vehicle – a two-man handcar to be operated by a pair of section hands. Two of the wheels were on a common axle that spanned the distance between the rails. The third wheel in the rear was in line with one of the other two, between which were two small seats straddling the upright pump lever with two sets of handles, one for each traveler. The twosome aboard this vehicle rode directly above one of the track rails.

12

A chain had been passed through one of the wheels and around a pillar that supported the platform. A big brass padlock completed the loop at the chain ends but the padlock was left open. Old Bill Mallaber, a railroad carpenter whose regular mode of travel was by handcar, had not snapped the lock closed. Perhaps he had no key. Perhaps he had abundant confidence in the murky obscurity of the hiding place. Perhaps he thought that railroad property was inviolable, unconditionally safe from all molestation. If that were the case he did not reckon with the exploratory spirit of youth. To Bruce and me, the unshackled handcar was an invitation to adventure.

Bruce exclaimed, "Let's get this thing on the tracks and try it out!" and with that remark we hauled that three-wheeled oddball vehicle onto the tracks. It must have been a formidable task for old Bill to have wrestled that machine onto the rails alone!

After a short trial run in both directions, we set off down the track in the dark of night. It was a two-person vehicle propelled by human muscle: we had to each take a turn pulling the big lever forward and then let the other pull it back. The action was a little like rowing a boat. Setting out from the depot, there were two or three rail switches that had to be negotiated by lifting the wheels one at a time before we reached the straightaway.

Naturally, Bruce and I were itching to find out how fast we could make this machine go. Youth and speed are synonymous! As we pumped faster and faster, steel wheels caressing the rails sang a rasping low whistle, joined by the clackety-clack of the wheels jumping the rail joints. Old Bill would have been envious of the velocity we attained, whatever it was. The blackness of the night augmented the sensation of speed. We were flying down the tracks into the ubiquitous darkness. The night air swished around us. The strange dark outlines of the near landscape sped past. Only the stars stood still.

To Bruce and me this handcar adventure was more exciting than a visit to an amusement park, and much more appealing to our egos since we were in control!

**The Hemlock Depot where Jack and Bruce
commandeered Mr. Mallaber's handcar**

The Water Tower
1932: Fourteen

One of our more daring exploits occurred after the railroad water tower was no longer being used. The round tank stood about thirty-five feet high, constructed of vertical wooden staves on top of four spindly steel columns. A flimsy steel ladder led up to the eaves under the cone-shaped roof. Near the edge of the roof was a square opening to the interior of the tank. Originally a cover closed over the opening, but after the water tower was abandoned, the cover disappeared, perhaps blown off by the wind.

Now there was nothing inside the tower but dozens, maybe hundreds, of pigeons. Bruce convinced me that we should explore the oversized birdhouse one night and count the pigeon population. It was not of great import to me to know how many pigeons lived there, but Bruce was my friend and I agreed to join him in his mission.

On the appointed evening we arrived at the tower with flashlights. Because of the questionable condition of the ladder we agreed that only one of us should be on it at a time. Bruce climbed up cautiously, reached the top, and reported to me on the ground that his flashlight lit up a catwalk suspended from the roof. He said he was going to lower himself onto the catwalk, but needed me to hold his flashlight since he required both hands for this maneuver.

Up I came. Bruce was sitting on the rim of the opening. I looked around him into the cavernous interior of the tank, sweeping the inside wall with my flashlight beam. There was no water inside, but the drop to the floor was at least ten feet down. The catwalk consisted of eight planks of about ten inches wide arranged in the figure of an octagon concentric with the tank. Pigeons were squatted on the planks at various points amid their droppings.

"Bruce, are you sure you want to climb onto those planks? Looks dangerous to me. I can't see myself crawling around in that mess. Let's count the birds from here."

Bruce took another look at the catwalk as both our flashlight beams scanned it. The birds blinked but seemed content to stay put.

"Well, let's see if we can count them from here," he conceded.

I've forgotten how many pigeons there were, but not the danger. If either of us had fallen to the floor of the tank we would have suffered serious injury and precipitated a horrendous rescue operation. Back on the ground Bruce concluded that this bird exploration was not one of his more brilliant ideas.

Bovine Memories
1933: Fifteen

Our barn door, on an overhead track that slid open or closed, was large enough to allow our 1931 Essex to enter and exit. Inside there was space at the side and rear of the barn, an area that had been appropriated as the bovine abode – namely a stall for old Popeye.

At her peak production Popeye manufactured about twelve quarts of milk a day. In addition, she exuded a couple of other products that gave an aroma to the upholstery in the Essex. This was not appreciated by Mother.

Popeye was so old she had only a few teeth. My father jokingly suggested we invest in a set of dentures for her, but concluded it was an impractical idea. As an alternative, he borrowed a cutting machine to chop up her hay, so he could "spoon feed her. "

Popeye was one of several cows in a long succession that came from our next-door neighbor, Dr. Trott. Keeping his cow in our barn was a business arrangement: he owned the cow; we supplied the shelter and the feed, pulled her teats twice a day, and delivered two quarts of milk to his household. We kept the rest of the milk.

Doc accepted cows from time to time as payment for his medical services. Although the principal of the barter was the cow, the transaction had a definite whiff of horse-trading. Obviously, a farmer was not parting with any prize animal to satisfy medical bills. On the contrary, the object was to foist upon Doc some critter that hardly would be accepted at the sausage works. In general, that was the kind of cow we received.

There came a time when we had to say good-bye to Popeye. Her milk production went way down and she was old and miserable. The morning the truck came to take her away, the thermometer registered thirty-five degrees below zero, the coldest day of 1933! When I awoke that morning, the water in the tumbler on the table near my bed was frozen! The linoleum under foot seemed to my bare feet as the surface of an ice rink. The biting cold must have been even more unbearable to poor old Popeye. I had pangs of sympathy for her as she passed the kitchen window aboard an open truck.

Cows came and went through the seasons. Their quality as dairy animals bordered on the ridiculous. One bovine in particular earned a permanent place in my memory. A short while after Popeye's departure, the doctor left a message at the house for me to lead a cow home from a farm two miles distant.

I started on my task directly after school. In the barn, I found a hank of rope about ten feet long and set out on foot in mid-afternoon on a sparkling spring day. I could hardly object to this duty in such inspiring natural splendor. I knew of the Paul farm, since Lucile, one of the Paul children, was in my sophomore high school class. I set out north along Main Street, then turned onto a narrow dirt road. In about half an hour, I arrived at the farm. Lucille and her little sister were in the garden behind the house.

"Hi, Lucille," I greeted them. "Do you know of a cow I'm supposed to get for Doc Trott?"

Yes, she knew about it and could hardly conceal her amazement that I was to lead the cow home. She pointed to the pasture where the animal was corralled. She stayed a few paces behind me as I approached the field of action.

The pasture was on the order of three or four acres; instantly I spotted its lone occupant. To my amazement this cow had horns! Most dairy cattle have their horns clipped at an early age. I opened the gate and proceeded cautiously toward the animal. Out of the corner of my eye, I noticed Lucille and her sister quickly closed the gate behind me. I advanced slowly, approaching Bossy broadside, looking her over carefully to appraise her merits.

When I was about twenty feet away, she reared, turning her hindquarters toward me. She obviously had learned long before that such a maneuver placed me at an unmistakable disadvantage. Trying to circumnavigate her rear end, she retaliated by turning, turning, always keeping that backside toward me. I perceived then and there the value of the cowboy's horse and his lasso. How I wished I had both!

I tried to approach her at various angles, but she either swung her rear quarters around toward me, or kicked up her heels and galloped away to another part of the field. I had observed enough to conclude that the cow's udder was non-existent.

Retreating back to Lucille, I inquired, "When was the last time that cow was milked?"

Lucille didn't seem to know with any certainty, but the conclusion was that it had been a very long time in the past. The truth was clear enough: as a dairy cow, she was worthless! But, nevertheless, my duty was to bring the animal home.

Lucille suggested that she could round up several nearby farm kids to drive the cow into a corner of the field. I was agreeable to about anything. I knew for sure that rounding up several schoolboys was much easier than rounding up one uncooperative cow.

It seemed no time at all before Lucille had acquired two boys and an older girl, giving us a team of six, including Lucille, her sister, and me. On the third attempt we cornered that ornery animal; I had visions of her turning upon us with those horns. Reaching through the fence, I snatched a handful of alfalfa and thrust it at Lucille, saying, "See if this will get attention."

To Bossy that alfalfa was like a cigarette to an addict. I passed a line with a slipknot around the beast's neck. I gave a tug on the line and we set off on our way towards the gate. Momentarily at least everything was under control.

I bid adieu to Lucille and her friends, thanking them all heartily, and with a firm grasp on the line started homeward. I soon discovered that, although lacking in those admirable features identified with a fine dairy cow, the animal had remarkable eyesight and discernment for the choicest green fodder. She could recognize a clump of alfalfa twenty-five feet away in any direction. Once spotted, there was no denying her intentions. She headed directly for it. I was no match for her strength and could not hold her back.

She advanced from one alfalfa clump to another, dragging me after her as a very unwilling follower. I was hoping that the line around her neck would choke her to death, but the noose did not faze her in the least. Our progress was measured from alfalfa clump to alfalfa clump.

Over an hour had passed before we came to the main highway. I was more than a little apprehensive about what would happen next. Would I still be contending with the cow's appetite for alfalfa? Would the animal cross the highway, oblivious to the fast-moving vehicles? My hands were sore and tired of hanging onto that rope, but I dared not lose my grip.

We made the turn at the highway towards the village. Not a stalk of alfalfa was in sight! Our forward progress picked up markedly as Bossy hit her stride down the shoulder of the road. The line around her neck hung loose – what a relief! It was as if she recognized that broad shoulder of the highway as her ordained route of travel! She was not fazed by the passing autos. Together we marched, boy and cow, into the heart of the village.

My instructions were to take the cow to a pasture lot on Clay Street, around behind our house. A fairly long, straight driveway led back to the pasture. I had a real sense of accomplishment on that last leg of the journey. In school I had just read from Caesar, *Laboria omnia vincit* ("Perseverance overcomes all things"). I had persevered; I had accomplished what I had set out do to, despite obstacles. The last steps to the pasture gate proceeded as a march of triumph.

I opened the small wooden gate wide enough to accommodate the cow and deftly untied the line around her neck as she slipped through. With some sense of relief, I hooked the gate closed and turned back toward the street. I had only taken a few steps when the sound of a crash startled me. The pasture gate came tumbling off the cow's horns at my feet. Bossy sped past me like the Pony Express, took a left turn onto Clay Street at a full gallop, and headed east out of town. What a surprise! What a defeat!

I didn't even bother to pick up the gate. I just turned toward home and the dinner that was waiting for me. Doc's cow was spotted a couple days later and returned to the pasture – but not by me!

The Handmade Boat
1933: Fifteen

Bruce had one idea that was truly ingenious. In the summertime one year, we rescued an old oil tank and made a boat out of it. His father, Clarence Wemett, operated an oil distributorship and owned the local hardware store. When Mr. Wemett changed oil suppliers, the new company did not require washing out the used fifty-gallon oil drums. The oil drums had been washed in a big tub which had been created by cutting an oval-shaped 500-gallon fuel tank in half lengthwise. The big vat had two flat ends with upward curving sides. The tub was about five feet from end to end and about four feet across, with a depth of about two feet.

Bruce's idea was to refurbish this half-a-tank tub as a boat. My reaction was definitely positive; I said that we should try it out on the pond above the railroad dam.

Jack's home on Main Street where he lived with his parents and grandparents

So, with a handsaw I cut a pair of crude oars from un-planed one-inch lumber. We purchased a set of oarlocks and attached them to the sides of the tub, one on either side at the gunwale near the end we chose as the stern of the ship. For seats we laid two boards inside, athwartship across the curved hull. The boards could be shoved fore and aft to accommodate two passengers, one at each end, or moved amidships for one boater centrally located. Of course, the bow was exactly as flat at the stern. This was not a streamlined vessel.

My recollection of how we managed to transport this "watercraft" a half-mile to the testing basin is vague. It was too heavy for us to carry, but we could flip it end over end. Somehow, we moved it to the creek. There we found it was exceptionally stable in the water – but only as a platform. As a boat, it was ridiculous! Rowing it provided excellent exercise, but very little forward progress!

We took that old tub out onto the creek many times that spring and summer. We even fitted it out for cruising in the rain. The second floor of the Wemett hardware store was crammed with obsolete, odd items of merchandise no longer for sale. There we discovered a large, two-colored umbrella that completely covered our unique craft. We had protection from both sun and rain. One drizzly Saturday in April, I caught seventeen catfish in that tub while floating around beneath the umbrella.

After a while, Bruce and I lost interest in the tub. The last I knew of our ship, it had returned to *terra firma*, being actually buried in the ground by one of our neighbors as a water hole for his pet duck.

Errands
1933: Fifteen

Every now and then, I would make the trip in to Rochester by train for some kind of errand. One such instance I remember in some detail. Anna Bush, a retired schoolteacher, was very active in the Hemlock Grange. Mom and Dad were members of the Grange. I joined when I was fourteen. The Grange was a farmers' organization promoting agricultural interests, but it was more of a social group for our family. One year Mrs. Bush was in charge of a committee for Grange participation in the Hemlock Fair. She had decided on a float to be paraded around the racetrack in front of the grandstand. I was chosen to be Uncle Sam, a central figure on the float and I needed the costume for this patriotic figure. Two trips to the city were needed, one to rent the costume, one to return it.

Any train trip into Rochester required early rising and trotting off to the station to climb aboard the train for a 6:30 a.m. departure. J.Y., the man who boarded with us in the early thirties, was the engineer on this trip. The train arrived at the Court Street station in Rochester at 7:30, an hour and a half before stores or other commercial establishments opened. In this interval I had to bide my time in the depot or walk the city streets. In the mid-thirties I put in a bit of time as an amateur sidewalk superintendent assessing the construction progress of the Rundel Public Library diagonally across Court Street from the Lehigh depot. I saw the large granite blocks slowly accumulate into massive exterior walls. Up near the eaves the stone was engraved with many quotations of philosophers, poets, and thinkers. Two of which I can recall, "Education is more than preparation for life. It is life itself." And "The shadows will be behind you if you walk into the light."

My route to the rental store for Uncle Sam's costume went through Washington Park, a small plot of ground bordered on two sides by Court Street and Clinton Avenue. In the park, destitute and wearisome victims of the Great Depression slept, sprawled out on the park benches and on the grass. They hadn't fully arisen to face another day of rejection and disappointment when I marched in.

They were ragged, unshaven, and ominous appearing. Had I recognized their number and condition before entering their domain I would have detoured around it. It seemed that all their eyes were upon me, scrutinizing me with envy. I sensed that I might be prey to be attacked, seized, robbed, that these derelicts' perception of Uncle Sam or of me was not one of honor and respect! My pace quickened. I scanned the more distant landscape for sight of a patrolman; none was to be seen. My pace quickened some more! Fortunately, no calamitous incident occurred. This experience impressed upon me the extent of human despair, and the magnitude of the social upheaval accompanying the Great Depression of the thirties.

The return morning train to Hemlock left Rochester about 11:20 and arrived in Hemlock at 12:15 p.m. The Hemlock train crew, however, made two intervening trips from Rochester to Rochester Junction to meet mainline trains, the second of which was the Black Diamond connection. The Black Diamond going east, train Number 10, was the first-rate daylight train from Buffalo to New York arriving at the Junction at 10:30 a.m. Its connection departed Rochester at 10:00 o'clock. If my errand was brief enough, I could be back at the Rochester depot in time to climb aboard the Diamond's connection to take an extra ride in car Number 36, the fast one.

On this trip we charged down the rails through West Brighton, Henrietta, and Rush with no stops. The rail ties flew under us as I peered out over J.Y.'s pinstriped cap. The train whizzed past the new River Campus of the University of Rochester. I had at that time, no idea that I would be a student there within three years. Another mile, and we sped past the

24

location where some years hence I would reside, in a house that would be mine for twenty years. And all that time living there I appreciated hearing the trains rumble past.

In Rochester, while waiting for the train back to Hemlock, another pastime was going to the movies at the old Family Theater on South Avenue. The theater opened in mid-morning and showed the same flick continuously into the night. The daytime admission was ten cents! On entering the theater from the street on a bright sunny day, all that was visible to the un-adapted eye was the movie screen. All else was inky blackness. I would have to find an aisle and then a seat by tactile means, stumbling against the end seats of an aisle. I could not discern the empty seats. One time I sat down in a woman's lap. Fortunately, she didn't scream! After finding a seat and adapting to the dark, it was a weird and comical sight to watch others groping their way down the aisles, fumbling to locate their seats.

On one return trip from Rochester I witnessed an unusual incident in Lima. J.Y. had released the brakes and we started up with the horn blaring and the bell tingling as we prepared to cross Highway 5 & 20. The road was three lanes wide at that time, with a center lane for passing. From my position sitting on the forward generator I could see to our left far down the highway to the east. J.Y.'s view in that direction was cut off by the cab's crowded interior.

As the train nosed out into the highway, I was startled to see a vehicle approaching at a very high speed. Rather than applying the brakes, the driver floored the accelerator pedal in an attempt to pass in front of us. The vehicle careened across the passing lane and the oncoming traffic lane. Whether we would hit the car, or he would hit us, was decided while I held my breath anticipating the worst. We made contact for a split second as the right-hand side of the cowcatcher struck the auto's rear bumper shoving the vehicle with sufficient force to turn it back toward the center of the highway. The collision could not have been timed more precisely for the preservation of life and property since the automobile had been headed directly for a utility pole.

J.Y. slammed on the brakes and the train crew, including me, jumped off to inspect the damage. A little paint was scratched off our cowcatcher and the automobile suffered a bent bumper and dented fender. The lone driver of the vehicle was in a state of shock, trembling, ghostlike, speechless. In a few minutes he regained his faculties, concluded he was still alive and saved by a miracle. We found out later that he was a salesman from New York City, obviously in a hurry.

The Railroad

*"The railroad loomed large in my boyhood experience –
what memories, what images, what nostalgia!"*

Grandpa: John Covey
An Introduction

To my grandfather the railroad was the key to life itself. In his seventy years between 1860 and 1930 he saw the great development of American railroads and witnessed their decline. As a farm boy growing up south of Buffalo, a career in railroading must have been as beckoning to him as one in astronautics might seem to a youth today. Years of education were not required – only the desire to start at the bottom as a fireman or a brakeman. Grandpa chose to begin as a fireman.

His first railroad job was on the Grand Trunk Railroad between Niagara Falls and St. Thomas, Ontario, about 1880. For a short time he and his bride, Emma, lived in St. Thomas. Sometime in the middle of the decade, he went to work for the Lehigh Valley Railroad. The line was constructing an extension between Sayre, Pennsylvania, and Buffalo, New York. Grandpa joined the construction crew. Working as a steam shovel operator, he dug cuts and provided the fills for the roadbed. Where the main line of the Lehigh crossed the Genesee River, he unearthed scads of Indian relics, arrowheads, and beads, some of which I possess today.

Upon completion of the main line about 1890, Grandpa's experience as a fireman and steam shovel operator qualified him to become a locomotive engineer. He drove locomotives for more than forty years, most of his career between Buffalo and Sayre on the Lehigh main line. I can picture him now in his two-piece blue denim overalls, wearing heavy leather gloves with large stiff black cuffs, and his striped denim cap with the long visor. As he sat in the driver's seat of the locomotive cab, his left hand grasped the throttle, his right arm rested on the windowsill of the cab, ready at any moment to reach for the air valve to apply the brakes.

Between Batavia and Buffalo the Lehigh tracks were level and as straight as a stretched string. To the north of the Lehigh road, the New York Central tracks lay parallel about a third of a mile away. It was over the Central tracks in that stretch that a passenger locomotive, Number 999, in the second decade of the twentieth century, claimed a speed record of 118 miles per hour. Grandfather believed that such a record was a publicity stunt. He took every opportunity to race Number 999 – or any other New York Central train that he spotted running parallel to the Lehigh tracks.

Grandpa in Family Lore
1915

My mother's brother, Uncle Ansel, told me this tale of one roaring ride his father engineered between Sayre and Buffalo in the spring of 1915 – three years before I was born. I've supplied some of the details, but the basic account is a legend in our family.

Number 11 from New York City was an hour and a half late getting in at Sayre. Grandfather, together with fireman Bill, climbed into the locomotive cab just as the departing crew was stepping out. The departing engineer who Grandpa was relieving, explained that an overheated bearing on a freight train ahead on the tracks had caused the delay.

Dawn had given way to daylight as Number 11 pulled out of the Sayre Yards headed for Buffalo, two hundred ten miles distant, with ninety minutes to recoup. The locomotive huffed and puffed upgrade along the Cayuta Creek for the first thirty miles. Grandpa knew he was pulling a long train as the engine seemed to be crawling rather than surging forward. He reached for his pocket watch in the bib of his overalls at nearly every milepost to make a quick mental calculation of his progress.

High above Seneca Lake to the west the tracks leveled. From his elevated seat Grandpa did not notice the expansive view of Seneca lake and the broad green valley. His eyes were directed straight ahead down the tracks that ended at the horizon. His ears were tuned to the increasing rumble and roar as the train gathered speed.

Back in the dining car, was a matron with her eleven-year-old daughter; the girl was admiring the scenery while breakfasting. The quickening speed of the train transformed the gentle sway of the car to a rapid sideways bounce. The ringlet waves in a full coffee cup spilled over into the saucer at the slightest curve in the tracks. The sideways lateral bounce increased in tempo and a rattle burst forth as some structural member of the Pullman vibrated in tune at a higher frequency.

The daughter voiced alarm, "Mom, aren't we going awfully fast? See how fast those telegraph poles are going by!"

"It's all right, dear. The train's late and the engineer is trying to make up lost time."

The waiters were putting forth an extra effort to keep their trays on an even keel. They gained some measure of balance and security by lowering the tray to waist level and grasping it with both hands. One of them observed to a patron, "Man, this train is really movin' now, sir!"

**Steam engine of the type driven by
John Covey, Jack's grandfather**

The tracks dipped down toward Geneva twenty miles distant. Grandpa eased up on the throttle. His train was roarin' now and concern for safety had to prevail. With some reluctance he reached for the airbrake control and applied the brakes sparingly as Number 11 thundered through Romulus and Willard toward Geneva. The rather sharp curve was taken at about seventy-five miles an hour, considerably above the speed for which the rails were banked. As Number 11 came to a grinding halt at the Geneva station, Grandpa had gained twenty minutes but was still seventy minutes behind schedule.

Thrusting his head out of the cab window, Grandpa peered back along the train to watch the departing passengers as the baggage and mail sacks were off-loaded. His eye caught sight of Gus, the conductor, running forward. At shouting distance, the conductor bellowed, "Keee-Riste! John! You threw half the passengers into the aisle on that last curve! Don't you know that an officials' car is hooked onto us with some high muckety-mucks aboard?"

Nobody had revealed that situation to Grandpa. He wasn't aware that some officers of the road were aboard their special car at the end of the train! He bit his lower lip and yelled back defiantly, "Gus, they know as well as you that this train is supposed to run on schedule. Now prod those baggage handlers. Let's get this train underway."

"John, the dispatcher says he's wiring ahead to hold BJ-4 at Manchester," Gus told him.

Grandpa nodded approval and withdrew from the cab window. BJ-4 was a daily freight made up at Manchester for its run to Suspension Bridge Niagara Falls. The slower freight train, once departed ahead of Number 11 would quash all hope of making up time.

On its way again, Number 11 sped through Clifton Springs and onto Manchester. The semaphore array on the approach to the Manchester Yards signaled a clear track. Grandpa shouted to the fireman to verify the signal.

"It's the highball, John," yelled the fireman. The expression "highball" originated in the early days of railroading as part of their signaling system. The signal consisted of a large white sphere suspended from a yard arm. The sphere could be raised and lowered. When it was raised to its high position it indicated a clear track ahead. Grandpa pulled back the throttle a few notches. Up ahead in the yards BJ-4 was poised for its journey with steam up, waiting on a siding as Number 11 thundered past.

Back in the passenger cars Gus ambled through, making his way toward the rear of the train checking passenger tickets. He wore that matter-of-fact impersonal expression that was characteristic of most rail conductors. His thoughts were of the officials in that last car, wondering to himself whether he should pop his head through the door and ask if he might be of service. It was a frightening thought to contemplate, for the officials might take a dim view of his intrusion. When he reached the last Pullman before the officials' car, Gus screwed up his courage and decided to enter the lions' den.

He opened the door cautiously and forced a smile as he cast his gaze upon three officials of the railroad. They were in their shirtsleeves gathered around a work table cluttered with business papers. Two of the trio were facing Gus. Mustering all of his self-confidence, Gus greeted the occupants.

"Good morning, gentlemen. Is there anything I can do for you?"

The more senior official spoke up, "Is there any chance of getting us to Buffalo on time?"

Gus fumbled for his pocket watch and offered, "Well, sir, it may be possible. We've made up quite a bit of time. The run from the Junction to Buffalo is a fast one, you know."

"Who's the engineer today?"

"John Covey, sir. He's been with the road since its extension to Buffalo over twenty years ago."

"He seems to be giving us his best."

"Yes, sir, and I'll see what I can do."

With that, Gus turned to make his exit and glanced at the large dial of the speedometer; it indicated seventy-seven miles an hour.

At Mendon, Grandpa slowed a little bit for the "S" curve. The passengers sashayed in their seats – first to the right then to the left. Rochester Junction was only a couple of miles ahead. Grandpa reached for his watch again. He concluded that Number 11 would be thirty-five minutes late at the Junction. Fifty-five minutes of lost time had been won!

At the Junction, water had to be taken on in the tender. While the fireman was handling this chore Grandpa marched around the engine with his big oil can, lubricating the piston rods and various moving parts for the last seventy mile sally. He was part way up the climb into the cab when he heard the air signal, two long beeps from the conductor, authorizing departure.

Fireman Bill had completed his task of taking on water and was shoveling coal into the firebox. He turned to Grandpa entering the cab, "What's got into Gus? He's in a hurry now!"

Grandpa smiled, "That son of a gun," he said, and stepped up into the driver's seat, yanking the throttle back a little too far. The surge of steam sent the locomotive drive-wheels spinning on the rails as if the rails were ribbons of ice. Grandpa was quick to shove the throttle back to its off position and then to pull back gradually reaching with his right hand for the valve releasing sand onto the rails. The drive-wheels found their traction and Number 11 moved out on its last and climactic run of the day.

Between the Junction and Batavia, Grandpa reached for his pocket watch every few miles and counted the mileposts. By his calculation, he was traveling between sixty-five and ninety miles an hour, adapting to track conditions. Number 11 sped into Batavia with Grandpa holding down the whistle cord. The cross streets of the city streaked past in rapid succession. Passengers on board for Batavia could well have doubted whether the train was capable of coming to a stop at the depot. Gus struggled to keep his balance as he passed through the coaches and Pullman cars calling out, "Buh-Taaayv-Ya! Buh-Taaayv-Ya!"

At the last moment Grandpa gave a powerful twist to the air brake valve. The brake shoes slammed against the car wheel rims with sparks flying. The passenger cars clattered and shuddered. The passengers skittered forward in their seats. Grandpa eased up on the air brakes just in time to bring the train to a smooth stop without a jolt. He reached into his overalls bib for his watch. 9:26. Holding the watch in his right-hand Grandpa took his usual position facing rearward, his head out of the cab window. Baggage came pouring out of the baggage car. Gus was in the background assisting departing passengers as they stepped to ground level. Bill sprang up and began stoking coal into the firebox to get a head start on the engine's voracious appetite for the next forty miles.

Gus shouted, "All aboard!" and herded the passengers for Buffalo onto the train. He recognized a regular commuter and told him, "You'll have a fast ride today!" Then he scooped up the portable step stool, climbed aboard and pulled the signal cord for departure. Grandpa glanced at his watch – 9:32 – and exhibited a slight smile of satisfaction.

Grandpa released sand on the rails, coaxed the train to accelerate rapidly, inching the throttle bit by bit to its last notch of travel. Ahead, the track lay level and straight as an arrow to the west. Back in the officials' car the speedometer needle crept upward to ninety, then ninety-five, a hundred, a hundred and five, a hundred and ten, and leveled out at one hundred fourteen miles per hour. The officials glanced at one another in awe. Grandpa and his train were in low level flight!

At that speed the engine's appetite for coal was insatiable. Bill poured on the coal as fast as a skilled fireman could shovel. His circuit of movement from coal in the tender to the firebox of the locomotive was a kind of dazzling ballet. The economy of his movements, their precision and rapidity were a feat to behold. Scooping the coal from the tender, wheeling around through half a turn, gliding two steps toward the boiler and landing his left foot on the air valve pedal, the firebox doors went flying open. His forward swing of the coal scoop was timed perfectly to alight on the threshold of the firebox door a split second after the opening. The coal catapulted into the blazing inferno. Springing backward with half a full turn of his body, he advanced to thrust the shovel into the heap of coal again, the whole cycle occurring in about fifteen seconds. The musical accompaniment was a cacophony of roar, rattle, and clatter punctuated by Grandpa's sounding the whistle on the approach to highway crossings: two long blasts, a short toot, followed by another long blast.

Up ahead, farmer Herb Hoffman plowing in his field beside the tracks heard the train's whistle as it crossed the rural road a mile to the east. Stopping his work, he folded the reins over the bar between the plow handles. Within seconds the train whistle sounded for the nearby crossing. He turned to watch the locomotive shoot across the roadway like a charging bull. The drive-wheels and connecting rods were a fuzzy blur rocketing westward. The engine's smoke streamed back over the passenger cars as if it were clinging to them. "That train must be doing ninety miles an hour or my name isn't Herb Hoffman," he said to himself. It was ninety, and then some.

As Number 11 conquered the remaining miles, Grandpa in the driver's seat was as a king on his throne. His subjects were all behind him – enjoying the ride! He wore an expression of determination mixed with enthusiasm, stern but with a barely perceptible smile showing through. Now and then, he interrupted his track-ward gaze with a glance to the north to see if he were overtaking a passenger train on the Central tracks.

Slowing down on the approach to Buffalo Yards, Grandpa examined his watch again. It was 9:57 a.m.; they were due in at 10:00 and had three minutes to make it! He reached for the cord to set the locomotive bell into its slow rhythmic dong, dong, dong, and turned toward Bill, who had only ceased heaving in the coal moments before.

"What do you know, Bill? It looks as if we'll be on time!"

Bill hadn't caught his breath yet, but managed a grin of approval. "John, you're a speed demon!"

"And you're the world's best fireman!"

Number 11 eased into the Buffalo terminal and came to a halt. Grandpa climbed down out of the cab with the big oil can and proceeded to squirt oil in all the locomotive's moving parts. Although he was six feet tall, Grandpa seemed tiny beside the great locomotive.

The passengers commenced filing past into the station. Some of them always paused a moment to pay tribute to that behemoth of the rails, that magnificent iron horse that pulled them to their destination. They admired the massive elegance of it all, the coal black locomotive with its nickel-plated whistle, bell, cylinder heads, and hand rails – a decorated black monster on wheels. Grandpa's mind was not totally on his lubricating chore. He was apprehensive concerning the reaction of any company officials who had ridden in their special car at the end of the train. They would have good reason to be critical of the morning run, accomplished at speeds far above normal and outside the limits for certain stretches of the roadbed. His back was turned toward the passenger aisle as he proceeded with his oiling routine.

Suddenly, a hand landed forcibly between his shoulder blades with a simultaneous jubilant outburst, "John, that was some ride. I'll never forget it. We have an important meeting this morning at 10:30. You saved the day!"

Grandpa turned to recognize the president of the railroad, all smiles and exhilaration. Grandpa's face lit up, responding, "Thank you, thank you, sir," and returned to his ritual.

Coming to Hemlock
1919 (and then some)

In 1895 the Lehigh built a spur line from Rochester Junction in Mendon to Hemlock Lake. Shortly after the end of WWI, Grandpa took the engineer's job at Hemlock, the terminus of its branch line from Rochester. I was a few months old. My father was in the Army in Spartanburg, South Carolina, so my mother and I came along to Hemlock with her parents.

It must have been a dramatic change for Mother to have been uprooted from the city of Buffalo and thrust into a small village that had none of the conveniences or culture of city living – no electricity, no public water, no cinema, no city acquaintances. One of my earliest memories is of a kerosene lamp at a low flame burning all night long in the bedroom. One of my first sentences was, "Go to Livonia to see the lights!" Livonia in those days had electric power and the streetlights held a fascination for me. I was nearly seven years old before electric power came to Hemlock.

Grandpa was a speed demon on the highway as well as on the rails. I recall riding with him in his 1928 Durant when he drove it for mile after mile as fast as it would go. However, he never had any mishaps or accidents because of speed. It was ironic that his only accident occurred while starting from a standstill in his 1922 Chevy at a complex street corner in Rochester. In this instance, Grandpa had no semaphore to indicate a clear track! Had the accident occurred in the era of safety glass and seat belts, injuries would have been minor. But the year was 1924 and Grandma's head shattered the windshield. Her kneecap was fractured beyond repair upon crashing into the dashboard. She was crippled for the rest of her life! This injury, together with my father's duty away from home for long periods in the railway mail branch of the postal service had some influence on my parents' decision to stay with Grandma and Grandpa. This was fortunate for me. I would have missed many of the rich experiences related to the railroad and a rural community had I grown up elsewhere.

The impact of the railroad on the village was immense. Employment on the American railroads reached its zenith in the nineteen-twenties. Residing in our village was every sort of rail employee: the engineer, the fireman, the baggage man, the conductor, the brakeman, the hostler, the track section hands, three in all, the station master, and the station master's assistant, and we cannot overlook Bill Mallaber, the railroad carpenter, who worked in Buffalo and came home weekends working the handcar from Rochester Junction. And there was Sam Boyd, who met every train. He drove a Model T Ford that he called "the stage" and delivered the mail from the depot to the Hemlock and Honeoye Post Offices. He also took any passengers who needed a ride over to Honeoye.

One of my earliest recollections of the railroad came about in a curious way. My grandmother was spring cleaning and asked Grandpa to clean the living room and dining room carpets. One pleasant spring evening he rolled up both carpets, placed them across the front and rear seats of his 1922 Chevrolet, set me beside him, and drove down to the depot, alongside the railroad tracks, then past the station where the train was berthed for the night. Grandpa and the hostler spread out the carpets on the grass opposite the locomotive. A long rubber hose with a diameter somewhat larger than that of a household vacuum cleaner was connected to the steam coupling at the rear of the locomotive tender. Live steam was then blown through the carpets. This mode of carpet cleaning must have been one of the fringe benefits of railroading, especially if you were the engineer or fireman! To me, as a preschooler, the long hose with hot roaring steam was so weird and frightening that I wanted to go home immediately.

In regular railroad operation, the hostler used that same hose to connect to a steam-operated reciprocating water pump housed in a small shed beside the tracks. Nearby was the familiar railroad water tower with the wood-staved cylindrical vat high atop its tall trestle. The intake pipe to the pump was buried in a steep embankment sloping down to the impounded waters of Hemlock Creek. A concrete-faced dam formed a long, narrow millpond about five feet deep. This pond was the arena where I and my schoolboy chums ice skated and played hockey in winter and boated and fished in summer. We didn't swim in the millpond, however.

The old swimmin' hole was at another location at the railroad trestle that bridged a small tributary of the Hemlock Creek, north of the Cadyville Road (now Adams Road). To one side of the trestle the streambed had been excavated to form a pool three or four feet deep.

When a group of us kids would arrive at the swimmin' hole the water appeared quite clear, but in a few minutes, it took on a chocolate cast, the mud drifting up as the bathers waded in. The more daring of the club, however, would prefer to make their entry by jumping or diving off the trestle about fourteen feet above the water. How the mud would roil as the jumper sank his feet six inches into the bottom goo! Not everyone dared to dive off the trestle. It required a very shallow dive bordering on a belly whacker, else one's hands might become mired in the muddy bottom!

A few of the older boys who were hooked on cigarettes would sit on the trestle with their feet dangling down, pulling their smokes and sunning themselves. One day the three-man section gang came down the track on their little gasoline propelled rail car. Pete Bartlotta, of Italian origin, was the gang foreman. He slowed down his vehicle as he approached the smokers and announced, with a tremendous roar, "You boys gonna burn up that bridge! You guys! You a-smokin'. Get off-a that bridge!"

There was an instant scattering of the smokers. Some leaped into the water, others scampered off the trestle. It was plain that Pete didn't sanction smoking. It was also evident that he fulfilled his duty as a conservator of the railroad property.

A Midwinter Ride
1926: Age eight

Riding in the locomotive at any season always fascinated me. This adventure in midwinter was undoubtedly more exciting than at other times. Assume it's a cold, windy winter afternoon. School has been dismissed at 3:30 and the train leaves for Rochester Junction at 4:15. After checking in with Mother, I set off for the rail station into the swirling snow. At intervals the snow driving against my face necessitates walking backwards into the wind. Visibility is down to about twenty feet. I cannot make out any familiar objects and suspect I may be deviating from the path to the station – but then, I catch a glimpse of the tank car on my right that's parked at the end of the main track. I'm halfway to the station.

I veer to the right to keep close to the track so as not to lose my way. The snow obliterates the rails and the ties under foot. Clunk! My right foot collides with a rail tie. I shift my course in this sea of snow to port. In a minute or two, I make out the rear of the passenger coach, its black exterior more visible than the rail station alongside. I break into a trot and endure the blast of snow on my face and in my eyes.

There is some abatement of wind and snow as I pass between the station and the two units of rolling stock, the passenger and baggage cars. Up ahead I can barely discern a human figure beside the locomotive. Sure enough it's Grandpa readying the engine for its afternoon run. Approaching closer at a slower pace I hear the sound of hissing steam as if it is leaking or escaping from a small orifice. I hear the mechanical rhythmic thumping of the water injector pumping water into the boiler. I hear the metallic scrape of the coal scoop over the floor of the tender as the fireman scoops the coal to fire the boiler. Suddenly, the pressure relief valve on top of the boiler section of the locomotive opens with a roar sending up a plume of steam that blends with the white sky. The roar of escaping steam predominates over all the other sounds. Grandpa, busy at this task, doesn't notice me immediately. I see that the big numbers below the cab window are 1804. That's the number of today's engine. Grandpa recognizes me and takes a few steps in my direction.

"Hope you're well bundled up for the trip today!" and with that he helps me place a foot on the first step up the ladder to the cab, it being about two feet off the ground and I have yet to acquire adult proportion. Grandpa climbs up after me.

Up in the cab, the fireman, a jolly Teutonic fellow, calls me "Sonny" and pauses from his coal shoveling. He knocks the coal dust off the bench at the left side of the cab where he and I will both sit – me for the whole trip, he only when he is not shoveling coal. My position is forward on the bench facing ahead with my feet hanging over. In back of me there is ample room for the fireman to sit. Grandpa is provided with a more elegant and comfortable seat facing forward on the starboard side of the locomotive. The cab is "winterized" by heavy canvas curtains to close the gap between the cab and the coal tender.

Grandpa inspects various gauges: steam, air, water. Before taking his seat, he shifts the slide valve mechanism atop the steam cylinders from neutral to forward. The mechanical system to accomplish this is huge. At the actuating end a gigantic lever protrudes up through the floor in front of the driver's seat along the wall of the cab. The lever extends upward five feet and can be rotated through an arc of about sixty degrees from its reverse position, through the center (neutral), to its forward position. For the engineer, shifting directions is a whopping physical effort. Grandpa squeezes the big lever with both hands to release the locking pawl and with feet well braced shoves the lever forward, steps back into his seat, releasing the air brakes. We are now ready and await the signal from the train conductor. Grandpa drapes his left hand over the throttle lever close to the boiler at his left.

The crew waits patiently for the conductor's signal to depart. With his right hand, Grandpa reaches through his jacket and brings out his watch. It must be 4:15; time to go. As the "Beep! Beep!" sounds in the cab, Grandpa pulls the throttle back a little bit. The locomotive accelerates slowly and silently before the exhaust steam is released up the stack with a blast: "Kerchoof!" Kerchoofs in decreasing intervals are expelled as the train picks up speed.

A little snow has sifted through the sliding window on my left. Straight ahead of me at arm's length is a window about nine inches wide and perhaps two feet high. My view forward is cut off on the right by the main body of the locomotive, and today the visibility straight ahead is minimal. Now and then through the blowing snow I get a glimpse of the cowcatcher. It's a good thing that this vehicle is on rails so that Grandpa doesn't have to steer the train on a day like today!

We chug along toward the "Y" where, on the return trip, the train will turn around and back into the station. Going out we'll be taking the righthand branch of the "Y" curving to the north through a ninety-degree bend. The first switch of the "Y" is open and Grandpa slows the train to a crawl as we enter the sharp curve. The six drive wheels of the locomotive emit a squealing and grinding noise like six tormented pigs pinned in a stone crusher. Just how the huge wheels manage to stay on a highly curved track is a mystery to me. Grandpa applies the brakes to let the brakeman throw the switch behind us to the left branch of the "Y" setting up a clear track for the return trip.

We move ahead with more squealing and grinding to the straight track heading north. We stop again as Grandpa waits for the brakeman to run forward along the train to throw the switch. I don't envy a brakeman's job today, braving the snowstorm, fumbling around in the snow to find the padlock, unlocking it in the bitter cold, throwing the switch, waiting for Grandpa to advance the train beyond the junction of the two tracks, throwing the switch back to its previous status, inserting and closing the padlock, climbing back aboard the train, his face and hands numb with cold.

Kerchoof! Kerchoof! Kerchoof! At last we're on our way. Grandpa gives the engine more throttle now. At increased speed the engine begins swaying and bouncing. It seems ridiculous to me that on straight, smooth rails the ride resembles one on a camel! I wonder how this machine stays on the track. Despite its erratic motion right and left and up and down, engine 1804 clings to the rails.

As we pick up speed it is increasingly apparent that the locomotive cab is more like a sieve than a shield from the elements. A cold breeze is circulating and I can feel it, particularly on my face. The left side of my body next to the outside wall of the cab is getting cold; my right side, a hand's breadth from the boiler, is heating up. It feels like there's a temperature difference of a hundred degrees across this little section of the cab! Grandpa voiced his concern that I be adequately dressed up; he might as well have said "sufficiently insulated" as I need the insulation from heat as well as cold!

We are slowing down now. The depot at Livonia Center must be just ahead somewhere. How Grandpa knows where he is in this snowstorm baffles me. Grandpa is applying the brakes; there is a chattering of the brake shoes against the steel tires of the drive wheels. The depot is on my side of the track and I look out to the left. There it is, hardly visible. As we pass by and come to a stop, I see what appears to be a sizeable snowdrift off the northeast corner of the depot. I know before we reach Lima that snow will be drifted into several cuts where the track is four or five feet below grade. The mailbag from the Livonia Center Post Office is thrown aboard the baggage car and it's Kerchoof! and Kerchoof! We rattle and sway down the track at a speed I estimate at forty-five miles an hour. In a few minutes we pass Murphy's muck land. I realize where we are when I hear the clunking sound the locomotive makes as it traverses the rail switch for the siding where produce is loaded onto the train in the fall.

We are approaching the stretch of track where there may be drifts. Wham! We just hit the first one. It feels as if a giant hand of nature has reached out to shove us in reverse. The train decelerates noticeably. The snow flies through the cab so thick I cannot see the window in front of me. Then, we burst through, the engine quickly regaining its forward momentum. In a few seconds it's Wham! again. A larger and longer drift. We decelerate more this time. The whirling snow inside the cab is so dense and of such duration that little piles of it accumulate on the cab floor. The fireman in back of me exclaims, "Sonny, this is a big one!" but then we burst through, an exhilarating sensation, that sudden change from deceleration to acceleration. It's a roller coaster ride on the flat!

Snow that lands on the boiler section inside the cab melts instantly, rising as a steamy mist that quickly dissipates. We encounter one or two more snowdrifts after which the big Teutonic fellow takes up his fireman's duty. I lean backward to look around the end of the boiler to see Grandpa. He happens to glance over in my direction and gives me a big smile, knowing full well that I'm enjoying the ride.

I *am* enjoying the ride, except for the extremes of temperature, right and left. By now I feel my left half is frozen and the right side of my body is roasted. If I could only average this temperature in some way, my travel would be quite agreeable. The thought occurs to me of turning around facing backward to soak up some heat on my left side and cool off on the right, but there would be no place to put my legs except straight out onto the fireman's half of the bench. Forget that, I decide; I am resigned to endure these contrasting conditions.

We are nearing Lima. I can sense a slight force tilting me as we encounter the sweeping bend about a mile south of town. As we get nearer the crossing, Grandpa may be able to see the Pinco

Insulator Works and its rail siding from his perch in the cab. The front entrance of the Pinco plant faces the main highway across Route 5 and 20. We must be getting close, because Grandpa lets loose the engine's whistle with a long series of toots. A motorist on the highway in this blizzard would be completely unaware of the rail crossing or the approaching train. We proceed slowly across the highway with whistle blaring and bell clanging. Grandpa doesn't let up on the whistle until all train cars have cleared the highway.

The stop at Lima is brief, just time enough to take on the mail then we chug on to Honeoye Falls. The track in this stretch is raised above the level of the countryside and there are no drifts to slam into. How disappointing! We back into Honeoye Falls taking the righthand spur of the "Y". More mail is taken on, but no passengers board. On our return trip this evening there will be the departing Rochester commuters.

Rochester Junction Train Depot

The snowfall is diminishing; darkness is descending as we leave the Falls behind and near the high trestle over Honeoye Creek. Grandpa has switched on the headlight and I can see the track ahead reaching out across the gulch with seeming nothingness below. I know the trestle is a sound piece of engineering construction but it makes my belly quiver. Out on the trestle looking down from the side window I cannot see the track. We seem to be suspended in space! I'm reassured by the sway and clatter that the track is still beneath us, we're not falling into the ravine!

It's downhill now to Rochester Junction and the iron horse is in a resting mode as we glide toward the mainline in the valley. Grandpa applies the brakes as we approach the Junction and the threefold vertical array of semaphores on my side of the track come into view. All three blades are horizontal barring our advance. We wait for the control tower to give us a clear track into the station. In a minute or two the lower of the three signals swings upward. The fireman announces, "Highball! It's the bottom board!" Grandpa releases the brakes, pulls the throttle and we clank and grind obliquely through several switches crossing the main line and arrive on the second track from the station on our left. The commuter train from Rochester will soon occupy the intervening track, the train that Grandpa and I will be aboard on the return trip. The fireman climbs down from the cab. Before making his exit Grandpa has to move the big shifting lever to the neutral position. Having dispensed with this, he asks me if I would rather go down the ladder after him so that he might help me. But pride prevails!

"Grandpa, I can get down by myself!" I say firmly. Twirling halfway round, I back down the ladder hanging onto the vertical railings on each side. At the final step I loosen my grip on the railings letting them slide through my mittens as I drop to the ground. That was easy enough. And I grin at my accomplishment.

Down in the snow Grandpa plods forward and examines the front of the locomotive. The snow is piled up on the cowcatcher well above his height. Still higher the snow is plastered in gobs and streaks right up to the headlight. The front end of the engine looks like it received an incomplete application of whitewash. The contrast of white on black is startling. Far in the distance to the northwest a whistle sounds.

"We better cross over to the station. Our train is coming," cautions Grandpa.

We step lively over the rails where the Rochester train will soon come rumbling in. From the station side I can now see the headlight far down the track. It is dimmed intermittently by blowing snow. Closer and closer, the engine seems to grow in size. It's a black, one-eyed monster, Number 1819, panting steam, wheezing, rumbling, making the earth tremble as it passes by and comes to a halt a little way down the track.

Glancing down I recognize two of my footprints in the snow ahead of me. I must have stepped back instinctively in the immediate presence of the monster shaking the earth! Grandpa has held his ground; he turns around and heads for the station with me trailing. There is no need to board our return train now. We have to wait for train Number 130 from Buffalo due in at any moment on the main line, on the opposite side of the station.

Inside the station it's cozy warm. Most of the train crew have formed a little circle just outside the station master's quarters. Bob Cotton, the conductor, is jawboning with Steve Farr, the baggage man. Bob, at six foot two, towers over Steve by nearly a foot. They remind me of characters from the comic strip, Mutt and Jeff. Their rivalry, antagonism, and antics often evoke laughter among the crew. Their ideas on how to perform their train duties are not likely to coincide. Grandpa joins the group and I overhear Bob saying that Number 130 will be fifteen minutes late. Deep snow in Buffalo has delayed the train's departure. I move away and take up a position to look out a window toward the main line tracks.

Grandpa has a daily domestic duty to perform in meeting train Number 130. It's a favor, a token of love, for Grandma: it's the delivery of one specially packaged newspaper, *The Buffalo Evening News*. The paper is placed aboard the baggage car in Buffalo and handed to Grandpa by the baggage man at the Junction. It is Grandma's link to the days of yesteryear, of life and times in Buffalo.

Outside, the illuminated switchman's tower across the main line tracks is the only visible object in the distance. Between the tower and the station, snow is blowing about, but there seems to be no new snow falling. Close to the station the electric lights beneath the long canopy bordering the tracks cast their glow on the windswept concrete promenade. Grandpa breaks away from the gathering of train crew members and passing near me says, "You may as well stay here where it's warm. I'll be back shortly." He's on his way to collect Grandma's newspaper.

I watch through the window as he takes a position where he estimates that the baggage car will come to a stop. The station master's helper, who had been shoveling paths around the depot, is standing by with the high four-wheeled cart ready to pull up to the baggage car door. Train Number 130 rumbles in, well decorated with snow. Grandpa is close to his mark as the baggage door opens. The first act of the baggage man is to throw the wrapped newspaper toward Grandpa. He grabs it with both gloved hands – good catch, Grandpa!

Grandpa wastes no time in coming back to the station waiting room. "We're running behind schedule, should get aboard our train," he says. As we approach engine Number 1819, I decide to run ahead. With one tremendous effort I jump up grasping the vertical handrails, squeezing them and pulling myself upward, placing my right foot on that high first step. Grandpa is amused. "Jack, you're just showing off!"

Up in the cab, engine Number 1819 looks exactly like Number 1804. In fact, any of these 1800 series locomotives all appear the same to me. I'm sure Grandpa knows them all individually, their small differences and peculiarities. Our fireman has the firebox well stoked and steam pressure up. We wait for baggage from Number 130 to be taken aboard. The Buffalo train glides out to the east on the main line. From my seat I watch the two red lamps on its last car disappear into the night.

Bob Cotton sings out, "All abooo-ard!" In a moment more he signals the two long beeps and the engine accelerates. We are commencing the long uphill grade to the high trestle, a mile and a half of roadbed carved out of the side hill. The engine buckles down to its task like an athlete; a long-distance runner that huffs and pants but never loses his stride.

I lean backward and look over at Grandpa. In profile his gaze is forward, sitting motionless as for a portrait. He seems buried in thought. Perhaps he is reminiscing about digging out this very hillside forty years ago, operating a steam shovel ten or twelve hours a day, boarding at the Tinker farmhouse just down the road past the trestle. I wonder what images pop up in his memory. I know that when the rail line was completed, he sometimes brought Mother and her brothers to Hemlock Lake on weekend outings. Uncle George has told me of such excursions and the various hotels and cottages that lined the lake. All of them are long vanished in order to preserve the lake as a municipal water supply for Rochester. I wonder if Grandpa's memories of these local experiences had much to do with his decision to spend his later years on this rather tranquil branch line of the railroad. Anyway, I'm glad he did.

Our train trip back to Hemlock continues. Past the high trestle we take the near fork of the "Y" and go into Honeoye Falls, engine first. Number 1819 crunches, groans, and chatters to a stop. I'm on the fireman's side of the engine cab, the best spot to observe the departing passengers as they will pass between the engine and the depot, and then disperse in three directions beyond. To obtain as wide a view as possible, I press my nose against the cold windowpane. There they come, strung out in a column, about two dozen commuters. There's Dr. Allen, my dentist, with his briefcase. This must be one of the days he practices in Rochester, the other two and a half in Honeoye Falls. If it was summertime and the window was open, I'd be tempted to yell a greeting to him!

In just a few minutes we're on our way again. Grandpa has to wrestle that giant lever into reverse, and after the train is back on the straightaway heading south, he must attack it again! This shifting exercise would be good practice for a heavyweight wrestler. The track, straight and close to level, stretches away to Lima to the south. Grandpa's zeal for punctuality is obvious now as he opens the throttle on Number 1819. The fireman jumps up to shovel more coal as we rumble and rattle at a speed of perhaps sixty miles per hour. The leeward side of the cab isn't quite as cold next to the window headed home.

We roll into the Lima station as if we were aboard a first-rate train on the main line. The depot is on the opposite side of the train. I hear voices and the noises associated with unloading baggage. Facing forward I can see that Highway 5 and 20 has been plowed, piling up two ridges of snow across our path, the nearest one only a few feet ahead. Grandpa sounds the whistle for the highway crossing before we start to move. Not a vehicle is in sight. The storm must have discouraged travelers.

I'm curious and excited now – what drifts will we encounter a couple miles ahead? With the snowfall essentially over, the engine's headlight pierces the night air far down the track, maybe a quarter mile. I'll be able to see what drifting has occurred since we passed this way about an hour ago. At a low level the snow is swirling in from the west. Far ahead it resembles a patchy ground fog shifting easterly over the terrain. Grandpa, of course, is in a hurry, not only to preserve his reputation for maintaining schedules but he knows Grandma and Mom will have dinner waiting. Whatever drifts there are we're going to sock 'em hard. Now I can see a channel through the snow, away in the distance. There's a drift ahead.

Our fireman, scooping coal, suddenly realizes that we're nearing the first drift; he quickly leans his shovel against the boiler and scrambles to his seat. Ba-Room! The deceleration on impact sends the fireman leaning into me. "Sorry, Sonny," he apologizes, "better stay put through these drifts."

A blizzard reigns again in the cab. The snow smothers the light bulbs but in a twinkle we're in the clear, picking up speed. The next drift is visible. Then it's three more in succession – Ba-Room! Ba-Room! Ba-Room! It's a good thing this engine is a steel monster to withstand this pounding.

The stop at Livonia Center is brief, just time enough to toss off the mailbag and perhaps a couple of cartons of express. The depot again is on the far side of the track. My view of Oscar Smith's bean mill, dimly illuminated by a distant street lamp, blends in with the panorama of the winter landscape.

Kerchoof! We're on the home stretch. Grandpa has only to blow the engine's whistle for two more grade crossings. If it were summertime and daylight perhaps he would let me pull the cord to blow for the crossings – what fun! Caught in the beam of the headlight is a little fox paddling through the snow across the track. The trestle at the swimmin' hole is just ahead now and Grandpa cuts loose with the whistle for Cadyville Road – who-oo, who-oo, who-oo, whooo. Mom and Grandma can hear that if they're listening: time to set the table.

At the Hemlock depot, we coast on past the second switch of the "Y" and come to a halt. We wait for the brakeman to throw the switch so that we can back around the sharp ninety-degree bend and on to the main track. It's taking a long time for switching; the switch is clogged with snow or maybe frozen up. I hear voices, and know there are other crew members out there behind the train to help. At last we receive the signal to move in reverse, grind and squeal around the bend, and then into the station.

The fireman climbs down out of the cab followed by Grandpa and then me. Grandpa has his dinner pail and he gives *The Buffalo Evening News* to me. As we pass by the baggage car, the station master's helper, Ken Coykendall, and the "stage" driver Sam Boyd, are sorting over the mailbags and express packages on the high cart. The paperboys, one for the *Times Union* the other for the *Journal American* are ripping open their bundles and shoving their newspapers into their canvas carrying bags for evening delivery. An elderly lady passenger is standing by expecting Sam to strap her suitcase on the rear carrier attached to his Model T Ford for transporting to Honeoye.

Grandpa leads the way along the path home, he with his lunch pail, I with the Buffalo newspaper in its brown wrapper. When we arrive home, I'll carefully slip the newspaper out of its wrapper, twist the cover into a rope and have a tug of war with Bonjo, my French bulldog. His official name if Bon Jour LaSalle! Once his jaws close over that wrapper there is no letting loose. I have to be careful, though. Mom doesn't appreciate my swinging Bonjo way up in the air around the dining room table!

Changes at the Railroad
1928: Age ten

In the late twenties the Lehigh Valley Railroad, as an economy measure, replaced the steam passenger trains on the Rochester branch with gasoline-electric cars. These were two-car trains with the first car containing the engine compartment, or cab forward, followed by a baggage section, then a small passenger compartment designated for smokers at the rear. The attached second car was a passenger car for non-smokers. There was no longer a need for a fireman aboard, nor a hostler to be a caretaker during the layover at night, a water tower, or a coaling station at the end of the line. The railroad was outgrowing steam.

In the engine compartment of the gasoline-electric cars the engineer was seated on the starboard at the very front of the car. He had a clear view forward through a large windshield and to his right through a side window. His field of vision to the left was cut off by the radiator housing which extended aft into the cab as far as the back of the engineer's seat. The throttle at the engineer's left and the air brake valve forward to the right were placed in the same relative positions as in a steam locomotive. One thing was vastly different: the shifting was electrical through a large rotary switch on a vertical axis positioned ahead of and a little to the left of the engineer. The crank or lever for shifting terminated in a large wooden knob. This whole mechanism appeared similar to the trolley cars of that era.

The major space in the cab was consumed by the propulsion system. In cars Number 24 and 26 two large Winton six-cylinder engines standing upright about five feet tall were each coupled directly to electric generators of waist height. The engine-generator combinations were positioned crossways, one in front of the other with the generator on the same side of the car as the engineer, and of course, in back of him. The engineer could climb aboard through a side door between his seat and the forward generator; otherwise, he would have to scramble over both generators from the rear door, opening from the baggage section of the car.

In gasoline-electric car Number 36 manufactured by Brill, the engines were larger and longer, positioned length-wise with a walkway between them. The engine on the starboard side had the generator forward; the engine on the port had the generator facing aft. In all of these cars my seat as a hitchhiker was atop the forward generator looking out over the head of Grandpa. I can testify that sitting on top of a large generator is hard on the buttocks! A pillow would have been a godsend. Car Number 36 was the most fun to ride in. Because of its greater power it could accelerate rapidly and attain speeds better than seventy miles per hour with seeming ease. Its engine compartment was very neat, clean, and roomy. The whole interior of the cab was painted a brilliant green.

The old steam-powered train arrived at the Hemlock depot by backing in from the "Y" and was stationed for the night with the locomotive facing west. It was found desirable for the gasoline-electric trains to come in cab forward, facing east. This direction kept the engine's radiator to the leeward of the winter wind. The water in the radiator was maintained above freezing temperature at night by opening valves to establish a hot water heating circuit with a coal fired boiler in the baggage compartment.

In addition, a set of steel overlapping plates about five feet long and eight inches wide was brought forth from a storage tray beneath the engine cab and applied over the exterior radiator surface. Two persons were required, one on each end of a plate, to place them one at a time over the radiator, building up from bottom to top. By the time I was about twelve, I had grown to a sufficient size that I could help lift the plates and secure them to the radiator. I took it upon myself during the winter months to be at the depot every night at the train's arrival to give the engineer a hand in buttoning up the engine's radiator. The most important equipment in dealing with this task was a pair of extra thick mittens. Those cold steel plates could numb one's hands in short order.

Another duty that sent me to the depot to meet the evening train was a newspaper route. Larry Button, the station master's son, and I took on the delivery of the *Times Union* when I was eleven years old. Larry delivered on the south end of the village, and I on the north end. My subscribers numbered about thirty; the monthly charge to each family was seventy-five cents, of which twenty-five were my paperboy's earnings.

Larry and I, along with the carrier for the *Journal American*, awaited the arrival of the evening train six days a week. In inclement weather, especially in winter, we retreated inside the depot where two potbelly stoves radiated their warmth, one in the waiting room, the other in the depot office. In the office Ken Coykendall, the station master's assistant, was on duty. He sat in an oak swivel chair facing the long built-in desk that filled the entire bay window projecting out toward the main track. By leaning forward he could comfortably look out down the track to his left to announce the train's arrival. In front of him was the company telephone at the end of an extension arm that swiveled so that the phone could be either pushed or swung away from its communicating position.

The telegraph key was to his left on the desk, located there, I presumed, to leave his right hand available for recording a message. Ken would demonstrate and try to teach us the Morse Code on the telegraph in between the clackety-clack of the receiver responding to intermittent messages being sent over the railroad system. When Sam Boyd, the "stage" driver arrived, we listened to his yarns about his native Honeoye; he always had the latest local gossip.

At times I spent a few minutes in the waiting room examining the posters and bulletins tacked on the walls. Most memorable was the "Railroad Calendar" published by the American

Association of Railroads. This calendar exhibited the twelve months of the year as one large display of three columns of four months each. The prominent feature of the calendar was the presentation of the economic facts of life of the railroad industry. Each accounting category of expense, such as wages, fuel, taxes, insurance, and utilities, was shown in terms of the number of days' income that was required to balance such an expense. Each category was displayed in a distinct color; for instance, fuel expense might have been represented by thirty days colored red. Most striking was the first four months of the year, colored green representing real estate taxes paid by the railroads. The profit (in the nineteen twenties) was represented by just two or three days' income at the end of December! It wasn't long after that that profits on American railroads became deficits.

The newly-emerging transportation systems – highways, waterways, and airways – strangled the railroads. The management of the railroads with its beginnings in the rugged capitalistic individualism of the rail moguls such as Jay Gould and Cornelius Vanderbilt disdained any government interference, regulation, or support. Historians and economists of the future will ascertain whether the near extinction of the railroads was a benefit or a misfortune to our society.

The period in which Grandpa grew and prospered corresponded with the crescendo of the American railroads. The railroad did not offer me the lifelong opportunity that it did to Grandpa, but the railroad, with its many attendant experiences, did offer me an exciting, enlightening and happy beginning. I learned many things from the railroad: about machines and personalities and their melting together; about attention to duty and punctuality. I reveled in the pastimes it provided: walking the tracks, riding the rails, diving off the trestle, fishing in the pond, and exploring the railroad property.

Ah! The railroad – what memories; what images, what nostalgia springs forth!

Changes at Home
1930: Age twelve

In September 1930, when I was twelve years old, Grandpa suffered a sudden and fatal heart attack. Two weeks later Grandma and Uncle George died within two hours of each other. My romance with the railroad could have ended then, but such was not to be. Grandpa's successor on the Rochester branch, hailing from nearby Manchester, knocked on our door one day a few weeks later, seeking room and board. Mom was not exactly responsive to the request at first, but then, she reasoned, we had the room and bath right off the kitchen that Grandpa and Grandma had occupied. It was ideal for a railroader rising at 5:00 a.m., gulping some nourishment, and hiking to the rail station just a comfortable walking distance away. Mom accepted the boarder at $20 per week which was a tidy sum in 1930 when hamburger was twenty-five cents a pound!

This new engineer was Jacob York Baker, or more well known as J.Y. to his rail companions. I quickly recognized in him some of the same characteristics and qualities that Grandpa had. We became quite attached to each other and I continued to ride the rails with him intermittently. On Sundays he would invite me to accompany him to Manchester to visit his family, consisting of his wife, and four daughters, all younger than I. J.Y.'s children came late in his life since he must have been in his mid-fifties at that time. He lived with us until he moved his family to Livonia during my senior year in high school.

Hemlock Train Depot

Vignettes of the Fair

"Mother Hubbard"
1920s

The Hemlock Fair has its origins in the middle of the 19th century. Agricultural organizations in Hemlock, Livonia, and Honeoye held fairs prior to 1868. In that year the three groups consolidated to promote a union fair. In 1876 the combined organization was incorporated as the Hemlock Lake Union Agricultural Society. The various episodes I have recorded occurred more or less in chronological order.

The fair in the twenties was promoted as the Little World's Fair, as there were no restrictions geographically for an exhibitor! Consequently, the whole gamut of farm animals from faraway places was eligible for competition.

Each September, a couple of days before the fair, a special freight train arrived in Hemlock loaded with prize dairy cows, pigs, sheep, goats, geese, and various other fowl, coming in from all the county farms. These freight trains were no doubt the longest that ever arrived in our little burg. I remember a locomotive known as "Mother Hubbard" pulled one of these trains. As the rail sidings filled up with cattle cars, the school kids flocked in to see all the animals disembark and then be herded or led to the fairgrounds. The spectacle was a little like a visit to the zoo or Noah's Ark.

One of the highlights of the fair for me was viewing the many varieties of animals on exhibit. And, of course, I – as did all my friends – got into the fair by crossing the dam over the creek, a clandestine route into the fairgrounds. In this way we avoided paying the admission charge. What kid would want to part with his scarce money to pay admission? It was better to sneak in and spend one's dimes and nickels on the midway amusement!

The millpond downtown Hemlock where Jack snuck over the dam to enter the Fair

An Early Lesson
1928: Age ten

"Right this way, folks. Three balls for only a dime! Win a kewpie doll!" The concessionaire's eyes scanned the midway crowd to zero in on his quarry. "You there, with that pretty girl! You look like a ballplayer to me! All ya gotta do is knock over the bottles. Nothing to it!"

The man's arm reached over the narrow counter waving three baseballs toward the young couple. The so-called ballplayer hesitated in his advance along the midway. The "pretty girl" clinging to his arm gave him a reassuring smile. His right hand slid into his pants pocket to fish out a dime.

The operator of the game was a young scamp, full of smiles. He handed the baseballs to the challenger, pocketing the dime in his soiled white duck slacks. He stepped to the side of the tent as the ballplayer took his stance in front of the counter to pitch the first ball.

The target he aimed for was one of two "pyramids" set up on a platform at the back of the tent. Each pyramid was an array of replica quart-sized milk bottles. The wooden bottles, painted white, were stacked in a tower – three on the bottom and two on top. The distance from the bottles to the pitcher was a scant five yards. It looked easy. Knock down all five bottles and win a kewpie doll. The little dolls adorned in glitter – and not much else – lined two shelves along both sides of the tent.

The aspiring pitcher loosened up his right arm and heaved a fastball that missed the mark completely. The momentum of the ball was absorbed by the barrier of straw bales at the rear of the tent. The boy seemed to be slightly befuddled by such an errant pitch, but the concessionaire uttered encouragement. "It only takes one ball to win a kewpie doll!"

More determined than ever now, the pitcher flung the second ball, knocking down two bottles. Only three to go! The ballplayer reacted with a smile, which he beamed to his companion. He gripped ball number three firmly, wound up and delivered. Wham! It hit the bottom edge of the platform, dropping to the ground. The ball was noticeably flattened into an oval shape. The three lower bottles stirred not at all, as if they were glued to the platform.

"That was close! If you were just a couple of inches higher, you'd-a had 'em!" exclaimed the operator. "You got the range now, Bud. Here, take three more balls. Only a dime!" He dangled three more baseballs in the face of the challenger who handed over another dime.

The target this time was the second set of five bottles on the other side of the tent. At the rear of the tent I watched the action. The operator had hired me that very morning at an hourly wage of fifteen cents. My duty was to pick up the balls and re-set the bottles, a task that a boy of ten years could aspire to.

The first pitch glanced off one of the bottom bottles shoving it enough to topple one of the bottles on top. The second ball hit the lone upper bottle near its base propelling it into the straw barrier. The contestant was definitely more accurate now in this second round. Again, it was two down and three to go.

The young pitcher, appearing confident now, wound up and deposited a fast ball striking high between the farther two bottles which lazily tipped over leaving one still upright. He spewed out a couple of oaths followed by an angry pronouncement, "Those bottles should have gone down!" He and his girl walked off.

It was little wonder that the bottom row of bottles clung to the platform. They were filled at their base with about five pounds of lead! My instructions were to set up the three leaded bottles on the bottom and the unleaded two on top. A light breeze could topple the upper two bottles. The baseballs were filled with sawdust; they absorbed a large proportion of the energy upon impact, leaving little to impart movement to the target. The contestant might better have spent his two dimes buying a couple of hotdogs and sodas, or two ice cream cones, such was the high value of our currency in the twenties.

While the young couple sauntered away into the crowd, I reset both stands of bottles, picked up the balls, squeezing the deformed ones back into a spherical shape. The concessionaire took up his cry, "Right this way, folks! Three balls for only a dime. Win a kewpie doll"

My attention wandered across the midway, where a weasely old concessionaire yelled, "Two thousand years old and still alive! You've never seen anything like it before, folks. Right this way!"

Weird and unearthly sounds were emanating from beneath the platform in front of his tent, the sounds attributed to this mysterious thing, age two thousand years. My playmate Harlan, in the employ of the concessionaire, was hidden beneath the platform drawing a violin bow across the strings of an old bass fiddle. I must say he was doing a whopping good job of creating uncanny noise. For a fee the curious could cast their eyes upon an old decrepit mummy. Perhaps the mummy was ancient enough, but it was only "alive" in the sense that it attracted the dupes walking the midway.

It's late in the day now. I've had my fill of setting up bottles, hearing the chant of the huckster, seeing the expressions of dismay on frustrated ball throwers' faces. I ask the concessionaire for my day's wages, about eight hours' worth. He sidesteps to one end of the counter beneath which is a pile of small boxes of cheap chocolates, tosses me two boxes worth fifteen cents a piece. That's my day's wages! The guile of this guy! If I were bigger I'd punch him in the nose.

That's the way it was, experiencing skullduggery both first and second hand. I resolved then and there forever to be wary of hucksters, on or off a midway. Yes, the fair was amply educational in a variety of ways.

Lessons on Display
1931: Age thirteen

It's another year and it's fair time again. I'm sure the motive of the school authorities in closing the school for a few days while the fair was in progress was not the idea that the fair was educational in teaching us the diverse ways of deceiving the midway patrons. Their motive, perhaps, was inspired by the hope of what students might learn examining the exhibits, admiring the prize livestock, taking in the horticultural displays, and visiting the school tent to take note of their displayed accomplishments. On the other hand, it could have been purely a defensive action, knowing that if school proceeded during the fair, school attendance would be substantially reduced. In any case, school was dismissed at noon, leaving the afternoon for learning at the fair.

It's Thursday, the first big day of fair festivities. School's out early. I go home for lunch and don my Boy Scout uniform in preparation for our troop's performance in front of the grandstand. This is to occur between the second and third horse race of the afternoon. I walk briskly to the fairgrounds, strutting right past the ticket taker at the entrance since the Scout uniform signals free passage.

The general exhibit hall is the first I come to. It doesn't greatly interest me, but I pass through it taking scarce notice of fancy needlework, crocheted bric-a-brac, knitted garments, homemade jewelry, wood carvings, paper flowers, ornaments – all handcrafted. From my boyish perspective these things seem rather dull, of interest only to grown-ups.

However, I want to examine the exhibits in the school tent more closely. I expect to find the school tent west of the Grange Hall, and sure enough there it is: a white canvas tent about 75 feet long with the main entrance halfway down.

The school tent exhibited the students' classroom work, grade by grade in the primary department and by subject in the secondary school. The teachers took considerable time to arrange the exhibits. Not only students' work from Hemlock was on display, but kids' work from other nearby villages.

I enter the school tent. Sunlight is diffused through the white canvas, illuminating row upon row of paperwork hanging from horizontally-strung wires. Under foot is coarse grass turf showing the wear and tear of human traffic. I feel like I'm out in the open, yet closed in, the setting feels unfamiliar, neither indoors nor outdoors. Every row of carefully hung student papers appears very much like any other: handwritten assignments and essays, blue ink on white paper, with here and there an art project from the students in the lower grades.

I must find my school's exhibit somewhere in this maze of paper walls. I search, row by row, passing mothers, small children, and grandparents. Entering the fourth row, I spot Bruce, one of my classmates, outfitted like myself in his Scout uniform. He's waving his arm, beckoning me to come toward him. The silence and aura of a study hall pervade this tent. Otherwise he would have yelled a greeting. I walk over and he points to a row of displayed papers remarking with a smile, "Here you are!"

Papers from our first-year high school English class are exhibited. There's a paper of mine. It's marked "A" with a 95 circled. Boy, am I proud! My handwriting is abominable, but Miss Rix must have been able to decipher it. I see that my essay concerns the virtues of Ben Franklin as he described himself in his autobiography. Next to my essay is one of Bruce's describing the character of Booker T. Washington and how he persevered in the struggle to establish an educational institution. Bruce's paper is marked 95 also. His handwriting is definitely superior to mine.

Bruce says he's about to take a couple rides on the midway and we make plans to meet at the grandstand.

I'm still in the school tent scanning the displayed material, noting who among my friends has their great works exposed for viewing. There's one of John Jones' all about the theme of the story *Silas Marner* commencing with the memorable lines: "In the old days there were angels who took men by the hand and led them away from threatening destruction; a hand is placed in theirs which leads them forth into a calm and bright land where they look no more backward – and the hand may be that of a little child's." George Eliot was a preacher all right, but it was not a very exciting story if you expected fire and thunder!

Farther on I come to the exhibits of the French and Latin classes. Miss Brau, our teacher, asked me to make a replica of a Roman tablet for the fair exhibit. The Romans wrote with a stylus on a dark wax surface, cutting into the wax to make lines and letters. They renewed their tablet by melting the wax. So! There it is! Inscribed on the left column: *Id est Romana tablella* and on the right side *Veni, Vidi, Vici*, a saying attributed to Julius Caesar.

What the Romans used for black wax was unknown to me. I melted a couple of purple candles that Mom gave me for the purpose, pouring the wax into two shallow wooden trays joined by a pair of hinges. When I presented this creation to Miss Brau, she was noticeably pleased about using it in the exhibition. Well, it doesn't exactly thrill me to see it here, but it does break up the monotony of the rows and rows of white papers.

The Grange Hall
1931: Thirteen

After I leave the school exhibit tent, I head for the Grange Hall nearby. The judges for the Grange exhibit are huddled in front of the booths, examining the varieties of vegetables, canned fruits, and preserves. The entries are studied carefully, but not one item is ever tasted! I suppose by tomorrow the blue, red, and yellow tags signifying first, second, and third place awards will be attached to the winning displays.

Beyond the judges' group is the booth decorated by the Hemlock Grange. Coming closer I see that it has plenty of material from Grange members' farms, gardens, and kitchens. In the foreground are all the fresh garden vegetables one can think of, neatly arranged. Smack in the center is a super-sized Hubbard squash from our garden. I know why it's so large. That sludge Dad cleaned out of the septic tank early this spring really made our garden grow!

On the left side of the display, on the third shelf from the bottom, is a jar of strawberry jam; it's one of Mom's. I know firsthand how good her jam is and seeing it there, it makes my mouth water. Mom's jam gets my vote for the highest award. I plan to come back tomorrow to find out the results of the judging.

At the Race Track
1931: Thirteen

The second race of the afternoon is coming up shortly. I'm under the grandstand, hunched over for lack of headroom. Above and behind me I hear the mingling of many voices, the yelling of the hot dog and popcorn vendors. I hear a grandstand hawker shouting, "You can't tell the horse from the driver without a race program!" Along with a pack of other kids I'm peering out through the wire fence at the racetrack directly in front of us. We can see the entertainment platform on the other side of the track, where a touring group of acrobats has just completed their performance. To the left of the platform is the bandstand and to the right is the judge's stand. which is a two-story structure, with the upper floor open above waist level, affording the race committee full view of the half-mile oval.

The sulky drivers for the 2:20 race have been warming up their horses, stepping back and forth in front of the grandstand. The drivers are garbed in their colorful flashy silk jerseys and matching caps. The sulky drivers sit, legs straight out, feet in stirrups as high as their heads. That acute bend at their hips looks uncomfortable and awkward to me – they look like opened safety pins!

It's now time to start the race. The judge looks on from atop the high stand. To his right at shoulder height is an old bell about a foot across. He grabs the clapper and bangs it against the bell producing a resounding clang. With his left hand he raises a megaphone and bellows a stern command, "Drivers, get your horses to the starting line." The drivers pull in their reins and wheel their sulkies around to head back to the starting line.

There are six starters and the track is not wide enough to accommodate six sulkies in line, side by side. The drivers must find their starting position as best they can, each jockeying for the best placement to give them an advantage. I note that the Number 4 horse has pole position on the inside of the track.

The drivers scramble for position in a hit or miss fashion. The sulkies charge ahead. The judge screams into his megaphone, "Wait for that pole horse! Hold there, Number 2! Wait! Wait!" But driver Number 2 does not control his horse. He has a sizeable lead and all the sulkies surge forward accelerating past the grandstand. The disgusted judge bangs the bell three or four times signaling a false start. The horses are excited, snorting and high stepping as they return to the starting line.

I hear the creak of rusty hinges behind me. Turning in that direction I see a small door at eye level opening outward. It's a door for a horse in one of the stalls beneath the grandstand to put his head through to view the outside world. However, it's not the head of a horse that emerges, but the head of a freckle-faced woman wearing a straw hat.

She asks, "Is Number 4 the pole horse?"

"He is," I tell her.

"That's the one who'll win!" she remarks, before disappearing from view.

The pacers congregate again for a new start. Less chaos and more order this time, as they get into line. The judge, with one hand on the bell clapper and the megaphone in the other, shouts into the megaphone "Go!"

And they're off and running! The sextet of racers flashes by us in a cloud of dust.

Due to all manner of visual obstructions, we juvenile freeloaders under the grandstand can see little more than the straight stretch of track directly in front. I keep my eyes trained on the race committee in their high observation perch. As they observe the racers around the half-mile oval they turn to follow the action. Now their backs are turned toward the grandstand, for the horses are in the backstretch directly opposite, a quarter mile around the track.

The seconds tick on. In less than half a minute the grandstand comes to life in a rising crescendo of yelling. The horses have rounded the bend and head down the straightaway. Number 4 is in the lead at the pole position; Number 2 and Number 6 are challenging him as the drivers urge their steeds to a greater effort. There's no chance to squeeze ahead of Number 4 as the sulkies pass the halfway mark and disappear around the curve. The frenzy in the grandstand diminishes.

I wonder if Number 4 will be able to maintain his lead. There's an outbreak of grandstand mania as the racers struggle in the backstretch. I can only guess what is happening. In another half minute we'll have the finish. The grandstand erupts! I push my head against the fence. Here they come! The drivers are frantic, whipping their horses and shrieking commands. They're thundering toward us! Number 6 and Number 3 are making a race of it, gaining on Number 4. The shouts of the drivers and the snapping of whips can be heard above the din of the spectators. The pounding hoofs flash past to the finish line. It looks like Number 4 by a yard, but we must await the judge's official pronouncement.

Shortly, the judge directs his megaphone toward the grandstand. It's loud and clear. "The winner: Number 4, Graham Hanover. Second: Number 3, George Bell. Third: Number 6, Max Migraine. Time of the mile: two minutes, seventeen seconds." That freckled face woman with the straw hat had it right.

Boy Scouts on Parade
1931: Thirteen

The race is over. It's now time for us Scouts to perform. Hugh Drain, our Scoutmaster, has arranged the marching routine. Years ago when he was a Scout, his troop paraded in this same formation that he has taught us. Today, the Scouts are to assemble in front of the bandstand. Hugh will hand out sixteen wooden staves about eight feet long, one for each Scout to hold upright as we march. We'll each be given a short piece of rope that we'll use to build our tower at the climax of our performance. As Bruce and I and my other Scout friends make our way toward the bandstand, my mind runs through the marching routine that we've been practicing for the last week.

We assemble at the bandstand and Mr. Drain hands out a stave and a length of rope to each of us and without much ado the program begins. The troop forms a single marching file and we remain stationary as the band strikes up a Sousa march – "Stars and Stripes Forever." We step up and down in place to get synchronized – left, right, left, right! On the command, "Forward march!" we start off on our right foot. Then after a few steps, the lead Scout makes an abrupt ninety degree turn left to march across the racetrack, then another left to march parallel to the front of the grandstand, and left again to recross the track. A final left turn brings us back to the point of beginning.

We halt in perfect formation. Now the line splits – eight boys at the end of the line wheel around 180 degrees and go back the other way, and the eight boys at the head of the line repeat our first maneuver, each file passing the other in front of the grandstand. At the corners of the course, each column heads diagonally for the opposite corner, the lines of marchers crisscrossing at the center of the racetrack. We learned from experience that this is a move inviting an accidental trip if all marchers are not attentive to their task.

At the turning points at the far side of the track the two columns march toward each other to the halfway point and form a double column facing the grandstand. On our next pass we march in double columns and repeat the same moves as performed in single file. When we finish, the two columns form four rows of four marchers and we stop, facing the grandstand – our four-by-four square of Scouts is complete. It's time to build our platform using the eight-foot poles we carry.

Each Scout knows where his stave is to be placed and where his short rope is to be tied in order to connect the skeleton-like framework. Of the sixteen staves, three are needed to make the surface of the platform. Charlie Wesley, the smallest Scout in the troop, whips out an American flag from his pocket, securing it to one end of his stave. We hoist Charlie atop the platform and pass him his flag pole. There he stands, carefully balanced, waving the flag. The folks in the grandstand let loose with applause and cheers.

Charlie comes down from his perch. We disassemble the tower and go our separate ways. Bruce and I march off together headed for a refreshment stand to get a bottle of pop.

An Unsettling Encounter
1932: Age fourteen

The years march on: another year, another fair. On Wednesday afternoon, opening day, I want to go to the fair, but money is scarce. I decide to sneak into the fairgrounds to avoid paying the entrance fee. I can get into the grounds by crossing the Hemlock Creek at the dam near the railroad water tower. From my home I go west on Railroad Street, past the depot, past the old gristmill, and past the railroad storage building.

I'm stepping along at a fast clip almost to the dam when I'm suddenly confronted by an unfamiliar sight – two tents pitched between the building and the water tower. The dilapidated tents are a muddy brown color; the larger one looks like a wigwam. A pockmarked old truck and a rusty car are parked in front of the tents, partially blocking my view.

Then I notice someone come from behind the truck and take a few quick steps toward the big tent. It's a woman. She's dark-skinned with black hair, scantily clad. She ducks into the larger tent and has scarcely disappeared inside before the canvas parts. A swarthy male face, grim and sinister, scrutinizes me.

My first impulse is to give this assemblage a wide berth. I quicken my pace, deviate from a straight-line route to the dam. I look the other way, trying to appear indifferent to these intruders. Are they gypsies? I wonder.

I hurry on my way to the creek. I skid down the steep embankment, slipping on the cinders that roll underfoot. Directly ahead the dam spans the creek in two sections, each about twenty-five feet wide, divided by a spillway at midstream. The yard-long spillway has several horizontal boards stacked vertically that can be withdrawn or added to for lowering or raising the pond level. Today the water is flowing over the edge of the top board in a uniform sheet, falling about three feet, then gurgling away in rapids.

I pause a moment to glance upstream. A hint of autumn is in the air. Yellow willow leaves float scattered on the pond. In the distance a fish jumps sending out circular wavelets that spread out and slowly die away on the placid surface. Farther on where the pond bends to the south I detect on the distant shore a blue heron maintaining his vigil, absolutely motionless, poised to strike at a passing minnow. In another month this feathered fellow will be winging it to warmer climes.

Enough of this gazing at natural wonders, I tell myself. I must get going. I run along the top of the dam and jump over the spillway, then pick my way through the underbrush along the edge of the creek, and emerge onto the backside of the fairgrounds as if I were a paying customer.

The Livestock Tents
1932: Fourteen

In the horse stalls behind the grandstand, the owners, the jockeys, the grooms, and the stable boys are preparing for tomorrow, the first day of races. Sulkies are being hitched to horses to be taken out for exercise on the track. One elderly horseman has a wheel removed from his sulky in order to make repairs. Another man is examining a lower foreleg of his racer. A big horse van has just arrived and is about to unload its equestrian cargo. All this activity no doubt thrills horse admirers and race enthusiasts but it holds little interest for me – I'm more interested in mechanical things, like cars and boats.

But I do enjoy seeing the livestock on exhibit at the fair. I wander over to the farm animal tents and pens. The poultry tent is directly ahead. I can hear the roosters crowing. I pick up the faint, familiar odor of the hen house. Inside the tent the cages are stacked two and three high, sawdust and straw spill into the aisles. There are all kinds and colors of chickens. I recognize white Leghorns, Rhode Island Reds, Barred Rocks, but none other. There are no labels on the cages for identification. Farther on are the ducks and geese. I know the Pekins and the Mallards but have no idea about the others. I wish I had someone with me who knows about fowl. At the far end of the tent are the turkeys and geese. When I get there, I hear from the nearby cattle tent raised voices, a couple of male outcries, cuss words, some commotion, crashing and banging noises.

I go into the cattle tent and I see that exhibitors are still bringing in their cows. My attention is drawn to a small gathering of men and boys surrounding a cattle pen a few yards away. They must be admiring a prize animal, I think. Moving closer I notice that the pen has been battered and splintered. A big bull inside has been on a rampage. Was that the commotion I heard a few minutes ago? His keeper is leaning over the fence holding a bunch of alfalfa in one hand. At the moment, he seems to have quieted down. Well, the excitement certainly drew a crowd; someone in the crowd spots me and waves me over. It's my friend Art. He's a few years older than me and has been out of school a couple of years.

"Jack, haven't seen you in a while. How you been?"

"Art, it's good to see you."

"Did you come in over the dam?"

"Yeah." I shrug – it's how all my chums get into the fair.

Art, with a twist of his mouth and a wink of his eye, inquires, "Did you see those tents over there by the railroad?"

"I did, yeah What's going on?"

"Well, it seems they're a bunch of prostitutes. I overheard someone say that one of the girls dances on a mirror with only a short skirt on!"

Art told me that Bill Fogarty, the deputy sheriff, was on his way over there to kick that bunch out of town!

My mind is in a quandary: what are prostitutes? That's a new word to me; I don't want to reveal my ignorance, so I just change the subject.

"Where are you working now?" I ask him.

"Work nights in the city at the Camera Works."

"You like the work?"

"It's okay. I'd rather work days, though."

I ask him about his sister Alice, but I'm thinking I'll have to look up that word 'prostitute' in the dictionary! Back then, youth was an age of innocence or perhaps ignorance, in keeping with the social and educational norms of the day.

To complete my tour of the farm animals, I amble toward the pens on the south side of the fairgrounds. The aroma of goat greets me; I see black goats, white goats, black and white goats, nannies, and billies, and kids. One adventurous billy is sampling a remnant of a corrugated box. He seems undecided on its dietary merit. The bleats of the goats sound like irate sports fans spitting out the raspberries. It makes me grin.

The sheep occupy the next series of pens. Their bleat, in contrast, seems soothing, pastoral and pleasurable. These woolly quadrupeds I suppose we learn to like as toddlers by looking at picture books. I reach over the board fence to touch their wool. The fleece is thick, dense and long. Already they are prepared for the winter to come.

I've left the pigs for last. It looks like the pigs have all had a bath. They look so uncommonly clean. There's no mud for them to root in either, just clean, soft straw. Some of these pigs are enormous, a heap of bacon and pork chops! What's going on in that pen up ahead? A big boar is climbing onto the back of his companion. Wow! But no success; he retreats. So, more learning to be had at the fair: today, lessons on the facts of life.

Hemlock Fair

A view of the Midway
1932: Fourteen

Thin crowd here today. Tomorrow the fair will begin in earnest and then the grounds will be well populated. This is an opportune time to ride on the Ferris wheel, my favorite amusement concession. With business being slow I should be able to enjoy a long ride today.

Sure enough, upon approaching the big wheel I see that only two seats are occupied. I exchange my one thin dime for a ticket. I wait for the operator to bring the wheel to a stop. He signals me to come forward up three steps to the loading deck. He plucks my ticket from my hand, presses down the footrest portion of the seat against the deck. I slide in, sitting in the middle of the seat. The operator swings in the horizontal bar, locking me in, steps aside, pulls the big lever engaging the clutch. The engine buckles down to its task, changing its tune as I swing out and up toward the sky.

Rising upward, I see the midway as it stretches out in front of me. It's the main street of a tent city. The big wheel slows and stops with a jerk. I'm at the very top. Another rider is coming aboard. The operator must keep this piece of machinery in balance by seating the customers evenly around the wheel. My seat is swaying and it gives me a queasy feeling. I glance down to study the midway.

Behind me I can see the merry-go-round as it spins, the calliope blaring its mirthful tune. Beyond the merry-go-round, the chair swing whirls, its chairs flying in a wide circle. On the opposite side of the midway are a couple of large tents surrounded by farm machinery. Almost directly below me is the Bell-Ringing challenge. It's a tall post with a round silver bell at the top. It's a test of strength to those who believe they can ring the bell with one mighty swing of a sledge hammer. On most tries the sliding traveler shoots up the post but rarely rings the bell. Whoever makes the bell ring will be given a trinket or a ten-cent cigar.

On the down sweep, I examine the structure of the wheel; it's a maze of steel angled spokes, spacers, and diagonal cable braces, all parts bolted together into an intricate puzzle. On the upswing I look for the concessions along the midway that I can recognize. I see the whole gamut of fakers, cheaters, and fast-buck artists that bring their games to the fair year after year. I reflect back on that experience with the operator of the "knock over the bottles with the baseballs" concession.

On the opposite side of the midway is another kind of ball throwing concession. The targets are stuffed figures that look like cats sitting upright side by side on shelves. They are set up so that it looks like any ball thrown at the proper height will topple a cat. However, the cats have a fringe of fuzz around their edges, sticking out a couple of inches so that a ball, unless striking in the center of a target, passes through the fuzz. The concessionaire can activate a concealed lever that erects solid pins behind the targets restricting their backward fall when struck. It's a no-win situation.

I can see a "wheel of fortune" concession, with its alternating colors and numbers on the big wheel. Off to one side is the "frightened mouse game" in which a mouse is released at the center of a square table. The mouse scampers across the table to dive into one of the holes near the edge. Those who play can bet on the color of the small squares surrounding the hole. Farther on is the big Bingo tent with its side canvas rolled up exposing to view the perimeter of benches and counters. I can't see from here the fellow with the lightweight chair suspended from a spring scales – the chap who estimates your weight after you fork over a dime. You can win a coffee mug or a small flower bouquet, if your weight is more than three pounds difference from the prediction.

Interspersed with the games of chance and skill are the food concessions. Fair food is one of the best things about this week: crispy, greasy waffles dunked in powdered sugar, popcorn, cotton candy, hot dogs and soft drinks. Thinking of food stimulates my appetite, but I won't be enjoying any of the treats, for I've spent my ten cents. Times are not the best; the Great Depression of the thirties is apparent everywhere.

The Wrestling Match
1933: Age fifteen

I'm at the fair today by midmorning. A short distance down the midway I notice a sizable crowd has gathered around a platform at the front of a large tent. I'm curious. Approaching closer, I see three men occupy the stage: a barker with a megaphone and two others dressed in wrestling tights. The barker is addressing the crowd, "Who out there will challenge one of these fine wrestlers to a round or two? Five dollars to any challenger that can stay one round with either Danny McGraw or Bozo Bonanno!"

Now, Danny McGraw appears to be a muscular young athletic type about six feet tall and weighing perhaps 175 pounds. Bozo Bonanno is shorter, plump, unshaven, fierce, and looking like an unfriendly gorilla. I think of Neanderthal Man. This Bozo could weigh 275 pounds, easy.

"Anyone out there that can wrestle? This is your chance!"

In the swarm of onlookers, I notice a couple of my pals, Bruce and Harlan, and make my way toward them. A college-age fellow who looks like a football fullback squeezes through the crowd toward the platform.

"Young man, are you a challenger?" the guy with the megaphone asks.

"I'll give it a try."

"Where are you from?"

"Near, uh, Batavia."

"Can you wrestle, farm boy?"

The boy nods. "I took a correspondence course on rassling." He's proud of his skill.

"A correspondence course? Ho! Ho! We shall see! Which of these wrestlers are you challenging?"

"I'll rassle your man, McGraw."

"For three rounds or less?"

"Sounds okay to me."

"What's your name?"

"Mason. John Mason."

The barker announces, "Mason, shake hands with McGraw." After a quick clasp of right hands, the barker continues, "Now, lad, go inside and put your wrestling trunks on and we'll get underway."

Turning toward the onlookers the barker harangues, "Now, folks, we have a challenger. This fight is for three rounds. Now, you will want to see what this farm boy from Batavia can do against our champion, Dan McGraw. Step right this way. Admission is just twenty-five cents – a great contest, a great spectacle for your money!"

About half the male crowd proceeds to ante up the admission and file into the tent. Bruce, Harlan, and I exchange wistful glances. We have no quarter dollars. A quarter to us is a mountain of money.

Bruce pops out, "Let's go round to the back of the tent and crawl under."

His last word is barely out of his mouth before we circle around the tent and dive under the canvas. We enter the arena undetected and are quick to join the crowd. About forty spectators surround the wrestling ring on all four sides. The barker climbs into the ring and informs the audience that he, along with the referee and a third fellow wearing a derby hat, are the judges of the contest. The contestants are exercising and showing off their muscles in their respective corners. The barker pounds the gong for the start of the first round.

Mason and McGraw charge out of their corners and spar at the center of the ring looking for an advantage. Suddenly Mason grabs McGraw's right arm and delivers the Flying Mare, slamming McGraw to the canvas. The spectators burst into applause. It's clear the challenger has the support of the crowd. The farm boy from Batavia is their hero.

Mason is able to pin McGraw near the end of round number one, but in round two, McGraw counters with a pin. In the third round both wrestlers are on the canvas exchanging holds, grunts, and groans but neither gets a pin on the other. The gong sounds. The three judges compare notes at the center of the ring.

The barker addresses the patrons, "Ladies and Gentlemen, the contest has ended in a draw. Neither wrestler is the winner. It's up to Mason to continue the challenge or not." He addresses the challenger, "Mason, are you going to challenge McGraw to a fight to the finish? Til you or McGraw pins the other, regardless of the length of the match?"

"Yeah, I'll challenge him. He's tough, but I think I can whip him," Mason responds.

The barker doesn't seem to recognize that there are no female onlookers as he speaks to the crowd. "Ladies and Gentlemen, we'll exit now and continue this match as a second attraction."

Everyone exits the tent. On the platform in front of the tent McGraw and Mason flex their muscles and exchange pugnacious glances.

The barker proceeds to build up the excitement and rivalry of the upcoming match, "Ladies and Gentlemen, this farm boy from Batavia believes he can win over our champion, McGraw. He hasn't proven it yet, but he's challenged McGraw to a fight to the finish, no holds barred. This next match will determine whether Mason is in the same class as our man. Both men are determined to show the other who's the better fighter." He increases the pitch, "This match will continue in about three minutes. Don't miss it! Step right this way for admission – only twenty-five cents for this climatic contest!"

Dozens of spectators pay admission and march into the tent.

Harlan suggests, "Let's try again to crawl under the tent."

We three hot foot around to the rear of the tent and commence our dive under the sidewall. What!? There's a guy laying for us. He's not one of the wrestling gang we've seen before.

"You kids get out of here," he yells, swinging his leg at Harlan's head which is only three inches off the ground. Harlan is quick to get his head out of harm's way and the three of us do some fast backward scrambling to get out of the tent.

"You might say we're not welcome," Bruce deadpans.

"We can stand here and listen. We can tell by the cheers who's winning."

The barker announces, "Ladies and Gentlemen, this bout is the continuation of the challenge by Mason against our man, McGraw. The fight is to be settled by the first man to pin the other."

The bell sounds, and some of the onlookers encourage their hero, "Go get 'em, Mason!" "Show that McGraw what this rassling is all about." "Pin this bird called a champion."

We stand facing the back wall of the tent, our ears tuned for the response of the spectators. We hear cheers followed by silence, then more cheering. There's no pin at the end of round one. Early in round two the audience is in an uproar. There are yells, "You dirty bastard, stop choking Mason!" "Ref, what the hell are you doing, allowing illegal holds?" Then, suddenly there's a wild outburst of cheers and applause.

"Ladies and Gentleman, Mason has won this match. He takes the prize money back to the farm in Batavia."

Then we hear the voice of Mason, "I'd like to challenge your heavyweight, Bonanno."

"Lad, you must be out of your mind. Why, Bozo will flatten you into a pancake. You can't be serious!"

"Yes, I'm serious. I'll challenge Bonanno to a first pin bout, same conditions as for this match."

"Ladies and Gentlemen, you've heard what this farm boy from Batavia has said. He's going to fight the great Bozo, a wrestler of international fame, a wrestler who holds titles in several countries of the world. We'll exit now and prepare for the next exhibition between challenger Mason and our super champ, Bonanno."

Bruce, Harlan, and I trot around the tent to the platform at the front. The barker is in rare form as he promotes the fabulous match between farm boy Mason and this monster, Bozo. Bozo is pounding his chest and appears to be ready to give an exhibition of bending crowbars.

Bruce wonders, "Do you have any ideas on how to get in for the next bout?"

I suggest, "What about each of us ducking under from different sides of the tent? You enter from the east end, Harlan from the rear, and I'll try the west side. If we all act at the same time that bouncer will probably only catch one of us."

"Good idea. But let's wait until the bell rings for the first round, when the full crowd is in there and the bouncer's attention is drawn to the ring."

"Okay, the bell for the start of round one will be the signal for the three of us to dive under."

We repair to our assigned positions, one of us on each side of the tent, and await the bell. The barker makes his colorful introduction to the match and sounds the bell. Instantly I'm flat on the ground scrambling inside the tent. All attention inside is directed at the ring. Harlan is first in. I'm a step or two behind and I can see Bruce on the other side. The bouncer is nowhere in sight.

Bonanno and Mason are cautiously sparring at the center of the ring. Bonanno appears a little slow in his movements, a little too cautious. Then suddenly as a stroke of lightening, Bozo thrusts his left arm under Mason's crotch, lifts him above his own head and spins him around – the Airplane Spin! The spectators gasp. Bonanno throws Mason to the deck – Ka-boom! But he seems in no haste to jump on top to go for a pin. The great Bozo is acting more like a proud cat that has just playfully tossed a mouse in a game of catch. He struts around the ring flexing his muscles. The crowd looks on, dumbfounded. Mason struggles upward with one hand reaching around to his lower back. He grimaces as if to say, "Ouch, my back!" But he recovers quickly, prances toward Bozo who faces in the opposite direction, puts one foot behind Bozo's right knee which folds as Mason hauls him down backwards to the canvas. The crowd cheers wildly.

The match goes to the third round as Mason is unable to manipulate Bozo for a pin and Bozo seems to miss opportunities. Again Bozo grabs Mason and twirls him in the Airplane Spin. This may be the end if Bozo can leap on top of Mason after the fall. Ka-boom, the timbers vibrate on Mason's impact with the mat. Bozo lunges for a pin but Mason springs away as if he were a bouncing ball. Bozo lands prostrate on the canvas and before he can make a move, Mason leaps upon him making a pin. The crowd roars. The match is over.

The Afternoon Unfolds
1933: Fifteen

After the wrestling match, Bruce, Harlan, and I go our separate ways; we've had enough of wrestling for one day. I observe a couple of planes flying overhead and notice they are landing and taking off from a pasture at the south end of the fairgrounds. I amble over there to the improvised landing field where there is an opening in the wire fence that leads to the planes. A small sign nailed to the fence post reads: "Airplane Rides $2.00" Just inside the break in the fence a fellow is holding a roll of tickets in one hand.

"Well, young man, how about a plane ride today?"

"It's a great idea, but I'm broke. Two dollars is a small fortune! What kind of planes are these?"

"Piper Cubs. They can seat three comfortably, maybe squeeze in four."

I stand there gazing in the direction of the landing area. Three men are walking up the path toward the exit. As they get closer, I recognize one of the trio as George Briggs, my Uncle Ansel's father-in-law. He and his companions have just had a plane ride, I suppose. Mr. Briggs notices me.

"Hello, Jack. Are you enjoying the fair today?"

"Yeah, it's great – a great day for a plane ride, too!"

"You know, that was my first plane ride!" Mr. Briggs was excited.

"How was it?" I inquire.

"Entirely different from what I expected. It seemed the plane wasn't moving at all. I asked the pilot how fast we were flying and he pointed to an instrument registering an air speed of 120 miles an hour. I couldn't believe it! I thought there'd be some sensation of speed!"

"How was the view from up there?"

"Tremendous view! You can see the whole lake and all up the valley. Everything looks so small from up there!"

I really wish I had two dollars! But a plane ride today is not to be. I bid adieu to Mr. Briggs and commence the homeward journey for lunch. After that I'm to return to the fairgrounds outfitted as Uncle Sam.

In the afternoon there is to be a parade on the racetrack, after the second race. Anna Bush is a retired schoolteacher who is in charge of fair activities for the Hemlock Grange. She has designed a float for the parade and Mrs. Bush has elected me to don the costume of Uncle Sam – to stand up straight and tall at the center of her creation: a farm wagon decorated with straw, corn shocks, pumpkins, and a bevy of farm lassies decked out in colorful dresses and fancy straw hats.

I'm honored to masquerade as Uncle Sam and think I fit the type, for I'm a skinny kid of six feet. I do lack the white chin whiskers and graying eyebrows. However, Uncle Sam's uniform comes complete with a self-affixing goatee. The float will be drawn by a two-horse team supplied by one of our Grange members who uses draft horses on his farm. When I return to the fair after lunch, attired in the uniform of Uncle Sam, I'll be allowed to walk in the main gate without paying admission. I'm looking forward to that.

As I make my way to the exit gate to go home for my midday meal, I hear the old bell on the dining hall clanging its call to hungry fairgoers. This year the Baptist Church Ladies Aid is preparing and serving the meals. A queue of diners extends out from the dining hall entrance waiting their turn to be seated.

At the end of the line is that wrestling bunch from the sideshow. There's Bozo dressed in cream-colored slacks and a red sport shirt. He looks almost human now! And there's the challenger, John Mason, and standing next to him is McGraw. With the wrestlers are three other men: the barker and the bouncer and the bald-headed guy that wore the derby hat. It seems odd to me so I join the end of the line.

The bald-headed one is talking to Bozo and Mason, "You guys could have had a better finish. George, your fall to the mat looked a little phony. Some of the crowd suspected something!"

"I know, Chief, we got to practice it more," Bozo says.

"Now, this afternoon with your match with Tim, why don't you end it with his pinning you in the Hammer Lock."

"Sure. We could do that."

Tim speaks up, he's the guy my friends and I encountered as the bouncer. "Chief, where in hell am I supposed to be from? Brooklyn?"

"Not Brooklyn – Geneva. You're the farm boy from Geneva. It's over east of here a-ways."

Enough of this, I'm thinking. I'll leave these actors to down a big meal preparing themselves for their afternoon show. Another lesson at the fair – nothing is what it seems to be, especially on the midway. It's illusionary; it's a world of deceit and make-believe.

Cleaning Up
1934: Age sixteen

It's Sunday morning at six o'clock, day is dawning. I've dressed, have gulped down a quick breakfast, and donned a lightweight jacket. I jump on my bicycle to do some fast peddling to the fairgrounds. The fair has run its course for four days and in the debris left behind I might find something of value – a pop bottle worth a nickel, or a dropped coin, or a lost prize from one of the concessions. There's no time to lose: I must be on the scene early before other scavengers arrive.

I pedal into the fairgrounds, arriving out of breath. How quiet the midway and buildings! What a contrast to the noise and bustle of yesterday. An orange-tinted sun is climbing up behind me. What splendor prevails on this crisp September morn. There's no one in sight to spoil the beauty of the sunrise.

But what's that odor borne on the southwest breeze? What a stench! The stink is coming from the excavation in the center of the racetrack oval, from the two temporary outhouses down in there – one for the ladies, the other for gents – that have served the fairgoers for the past four days. Whoooey! I pounce on the bike pedals and turn south to reach some untainted air.

Along the midway litter is scattered everywhere – paper cups, napkins, posters, programs, half-eaten hot dogs, fragments of ice cream cones, popcorn boxes, candy wrappers, advertising circulars. Yesterday, the midway was an avenue of tents jammed with humanity. Today, the few tents that remain will be gone by midday. The area is a wasteland of rubbish scattered far afield, empty of inhabitants.

I dismount, push the bicycle along while looking down, examining the well-worn turf of the midway. All I see is a mess of pop bottle caps looking like dropped coins. After a few minutes of this search I'm about to admit defeat, then in the higher grass where the "swing the sledge hammer – ring the bell" concession was set up I spot a foil-wrapped ten-cent cigar, totally preserved – a Dutch Master Perfecto. Such a prize has no personal value to me but I'll give it to Dad to pass on to one of his card-playing buddies.

Farther on toward the grandstand my eye catches the glimmer of a pop bottle. I pick up the bottle and put it into the wire basket attached to the bicycle handlebars. Up ahead of me now is the south end of the grandstand and ticket booth. The ground in between is well littered with half torn tickets and discarded race programs. I lean the bike against the top rail of the racetrack fence and climb the short flight of steps into the grandstand. The tiers of foot high steps serving as seating are littered with oodles of paper trash. I scurry up and down the high steps crisscrossing the grandstand from end to end looking for some token of value. The exploration appears unrewarding, but then on the north side almost to the top tier of seating, lying prone is that familiar green hourglass-shaped Coca-Cola bottle – another nickel. This brings my total treasure hunt profit to twenty cents.

I hear footsteps behind me and turn around to see Bruce climbing up.

"You beat me to it," he says. "I noticed your bike down there with the pop bottle and now you've got another one."

"I got up extra early to be here. What's your luck? Found anything?"

"One bottle that I hid near a post along the track. I'll pick it up on my way out."

"Well, there doesn't seem to be anything else here of value. Let's go up on the roof and look around."

Bruce and I make our way toward the opening in the roof in the uppermost tier of risers. We've made this climb before. The opening through the roof is about three feet square. I spring up through the hole and crawl onto the roof. Bruce follows, and we stand up.

The roof slopes gradually upward toward the center ridge, then slopes down to the front eaves. The area of the roof where we're standing is emblazoned with brilliant yellow letters about twenty feet high spelling out HEMLOCK. Under the name in the same color and stretching nearly the full length of the grandstand is an arrow pointing to the airport a mile away to the north.

Bruce and I walk up the slope to the ridge in the center of the roof. Standing at the peak facing east we have a bird's eye view of the whole fairgrounds and the village beyond. Houses are hidden behind the trees lining Main Street, trees decked out in their fall foliage. The brilliant morning sun intensifies the hues of red and yellow and orange. On our left a dense band of willows conceals the Hemlock Creek as it curves around the north end of the fairgrounds.

In front of us the racetrack oval encompasses the baseball diamond where both our school and town teams have met their rivals. To our right, remnants of the midway are still apparent, and beyond the fairgrounds stretch a series of fields and vineyards southward toward the lake. In every direction images come to mind of earlier experiences. This panorama before me signifies home. I have a keen sense of place, of belonging.

The fair this year is over; it's history. I enjoyed it all: the camaraderie of my pals, the "educational" experience of adding to my vocabulary, and the observation of mankind's trickeries. Where will Bruce and I be at this time next year, I wonder. By June, both of us will have graduated from high school and be departing for places unknown. It's unlikely that either of us will be here for the fair next year – or in future years. If we do return, the fair will never be the same for us. It will have lost its fostering influence, its subtle power to teach us about life and people, its power to shape our characters.

What Happened Next

Jack graduated from Hemlock High School in June 1935 at the top of his class. In the fall he enrolled in college. He graduated from the University of Rochester in 1939 with a Bachelor of Science degree. For a few years he worked for Eastman Kodak, then for a time at the U of R.

In the summer of 1942 he married Madlyn Horacek; they made their home in Monroe County, where their five children were born: Randy, Paul, Alayne, Karen, and Mitchel.

Jack co-founded Tropel Corporation in Fairport in the nineteen-fifties, then in 1967 established a new optics company in Bloomfield: Velmex, Inc., which manufactured "dovetail slides" used by laboratories and optical instrument makers.

In 1983 Velmex purchased the empty Hemlock school building, with a possible plan to relocate the business to Hemlock. Toward that goal, the building was renovated, adding a new heating system, windows, and doors. The proposal to move Velmex, however, was never realized, and Jack donated the building to Livonia Township in 1996. The once-busy classrooms were leased to various community groups.

Livonia closed the building in November of 2016. A short while a later a group of twenty or so town residents formed the Little Lakes Community Association. They purchased the building from the town of Livonia and organized a Community Center.

Hemlock School, where Jack started school; the building burned in the summer of 1928 and was replaced on the same site the following spring

Hemlock School where Jack attended after 1929; today the Little Finger Lakes Center

www.ingramcontent.com/pod-product-compliance
Lightning Source LLC
Chambersburg PA
CBHW031223120626
46545CB00003B/966